Tabloid
Tokyo

Tabloid Tokyo

101 Tales of Sex, Crime and the Bizarre from Japan's Wild Weeklies

by

Geoff Botting
Ryann Connell
Michael Hoffman
Mark Schreiber

Illustrations by

Hirosuke "Amore" Ueno

KODANSHA INTERNATIONAL
Tokyo · New York · London

Distributed in the United States by Kodansha America Inc., and in the United Kingdom and continental Europe by Kodansha Europe Ltd.

Published by Kodansha International Ltd., 17–14 Otowa 1-chome, Bunkyo-ku, Tokyo 112–8652, and Kodansha America, Inc.

ISBN-13: 978–4–7700–2892–1
ISBN-10: 4–7700–2892–X

First edition, 2005
10 09 08 07 06 05   10 9 8 7 6 5 4 3 2 1

www.kodansha-intl.com

Contents

PREFACE

"Looking up the skirts of young women . . ."

Thus begins our first tale of tabloid Tokyo. So, reader—just what are you getting yourself into?

Into deep waters for sure, though perverted voyeurs are not our main characters, nor is perverted voyeurism our theme. *Tabloid Tokyo* is, first and foremost, a book about Japan—the Japan that lurks beneath the conventional images of cherry blossoms, inscrutable ambiguity, economic predators and any other cliche you may have heard.

Is *Tabloid Tokyo*'s Japan, then, the "real" Japan? That would be a bold claim indeed for an anthology of stories with titles like "Pornographers Target Public Baths," "Moms Mistake Kids for Pets," and "End of World Found in Tokyo."

Not *the* real Japan, but certainly *a* real Japan, or a *part* of the real Japan. True, there is more to these islands than falls within our purview—though the nooks and crannies we peer into would comprise a fairly vast area if laid end to end. The weird characters, uncanny situations, bizarre relationships and stressed-out states of mind you will encounter in these pages are as real as anything imaginable, and no understanding of Japan—or of humanity, for that matter—is complete without taking their measure.

The stories in this book were originally written for the "Tokyo Confidential" column of the *Japan Times* and the "Waiwai" section of the online *Mainichi Daily News*. Every week brings forth a fresh crop of them, each one an unexpected and illuminating take on this most unusual of advanced countries.

Where, it will be asked, do we seek this unexpected illumination? Answer: In "the weeklies."

We call them that, though some of the 15-odd Japanese magazines we use as sources are bi-weeklies and monthlies. An unimportant detail. They are alike in spirit, the spirit being feisty, inquiring and, with a nod and a smirk to those who reflexively attach the adjective "buttoned-down" to Japan, uninhibited—occasionally shockingly so.

Japan's newsmagazines—or if that's too dignified a term, its tabloids—are in stark contrast to the notoriously staid daily press. Newspapers, constrained by a cozy "press club" system into functioning as allies rather than, as in most of the West, natural adversaries of the powers that be, toe a generally deferential and polite line. The weeklies, excluded from the press clubs, scorn politeness, defer to no one, and thumb their noses at social convention— sometimes even at the law, seeming at times almost to court legal challenges—in the primary interest of a good story, regardless of whose chicanery or peccadilloes it may expose, or what unpleasantness it may lay bare.

The weeklies have eyes everywhere—in restaurants, offices, bars, nursing homes, private homes, bathhouses, bathrooms, classrooms, bedrooms, wombs, tombs, sex shops, pet shops . . . They are the ubiquitous flies on the wall, and proud of it. Like newsmagazines everywhere, they cover politics, business, sports, science and entertainment. But they are at their best writing about daily life and the secrets teeming beneath its surface ordinariness. That, above all, is what we look for in them.

If a good story is primary, what of truth? Is it secondary? Do the Mr. A's, Ms. B's and assorted pseudonymously named characters who populate the more lurid tales of sexual (or sexless) trends really exist?

We can't swear to it, but we believe they do, though perhaps a measure of exaggeration should be allowed for. It is the nature of a good story to grow better in the telling. We believe they essentially exist as portrayed because they are credible. As long-term residents of this country, we know people like them. Sometimes we *are* people like them.

Michael Hoffman

NOTE: Japanese names are given in the Western order, given name first, family name second. The names of non-public figures are likely to be pseudonyms. The value of the Yen has varied during the years covered by these stories. At the time of printing, the exchange rate was hovering around ¥100 to $1, which simplifies calculating (i.e. ¥1000 equals $10; ¥10,000 equals $100; ¥1 million equals $10,0000; and so on.)

PANTY-GAZING RESEARCH REVEALED

Shukan Gendai (March 30, 2002)

Looking up the skirts of young women has long been an obsession among Japanese men, as anyone knows, thanks to the plethora of books, magazines and websites devoted to panty viewing. On the streets, young women wearing short skirts need to be on guard for countless Peeping Toms angling for a furtive glimpse or two. There is even a common word in Japanese for catching a glimpse of a woman's panties—*panchira*.

Shoichi Inoue, a sociologist at the International Research Center for Japanese Studies, finds this all very strange, he tells *Shukan Gendai*. Inoue recalls a conversation in the 1980s with a Chinese student studying in Japan, who was baffled by the elaborate efforts of young Japanese women to hold down their hems while climbing stairs in public places. When told the women were trying to prevent their panties from being exposed, the student replied, "So what's to be ashamed about?"

What indeed. Inoue recently decided to thoroughly research Japan's "panchira culture." He wanted to figure out why the sight of a pair of women's panties can have an almost mystical hold on some men.

His research took him back to the early Showa Era, which began in 1926, when Japanese women first started wearing Western-style undergarments. "Already there were men seeking a glimpse of women's underwear," Inoue says. "They were few in number but they existed nevertheless and they were generally treated as weirdos."

But in the 1960s, that decade of turmoil and radical change, the proclivity became viewed as "normal," he says. "The magazines of the time have articles telling the best places where panties could be viewed," he says. Favorite spots included construction sites, where there were good chances that high-heeled and mini-skirted pedestrians would trip over debris and fall down, thereby providing panchira geeks with million-dollar views.

"It was a gradual process, but we started seeing the birth of an attitude in the '60s in which panchira was something to be enjoyed," Inoue says. As for the reasons behind this particular obsession, Inoue's theory underscores the influence of Japan's high rates of economic growth throughout much of the postwar period. "This [boom] gave the Japanese people a middle-class mentality and an excessive desire to follow foreign culture and lifestyle. I believe that this was when Japan's panchira culture began to bloom," he says.

"One aspect of the excessive adoption of Western culture was that women developed an extremely strong sense of shame. Not wanting to be inferior to Western women, they became unusually conscientious in not letting their panties be seen," Inoue says.

As for the effect this had on men . . . Well, men, Inoue points out, are only human. And it is human nature to want a peek of anything that others go to great lengths to keep hidden from view.

As for Inoue, he likens an unexpected glimpse up the skirt of an attractive woman to finding a ¥100 coin on the street. "It doesn't make me really, really happy. But if you're a man, it can in some way be an enriching experience." (GB)

YOUNGER TEENS DISCOVER SEX

Spa! (July 23, 2002)

"My impression," says a gynecologist offering free weekly health consultations in Tokyo's Roppongi district, "is that 30 percent of junior high school students have had a sexual experience by the time they graduate."

"We get phone calls from neighborhood love hotels," says a junior high school principal. "'A student of yours was here and didn't pay—would you kindly assume responsibility?'"

"Just recently," says a junior high school guidance counselor, "a couple that had graduated this spring dropped by for a visit—with their 2-month-old baby!"

"It sure wasn't like this in my day," older readers will be muttering. No indeed. But sex, says *Spa!*, is now firmly embedded in the lives of the under-15 set.

For better, or for worse? When sex was repressed, liberation seemed the key to happiness. And 14-year-old Kana-chan, spotted by the magazine on her way home from a Shibuya shopping spree, does seem happy. She finally lost her virginity in June after "near-sex experiences" with 10 boyfriends.

Well, why not, if it feels good? Disease and pregnancy are two obvious objections. "Kids are having sex before they know much about it," says Tsuneo Akaeda, the Roppongi health adviser. Precautions are not uppermost in their minds. What child, excited over a new toy, pauses to read the instructions? Akaeda sees a connection between instant sex and instant food. Both emphasize quantity and convenience over quality. Both implicitly pose the question of whether something so readily at hand is worth anything at all.

And both, Akaeda continues, imply a deteriorating family environment. With mom's life no longer centered on the home and dad no more available than he was when mom's presence was taken for granted, many kids grow up adequately fed but emotionally undernourished. Anxious and timid, craving acceptance and fearing dislike, they reach puberty seeking in sex the "skinship" they missed as children. Girls are particularly vulnerable, the adviser believes. The intensity of a boy's desire is both flattering and menacing, threatening a stinging rebuff if thwarted.

Spa! acknowledges that the media may not be helping matters. Casual teen sex makes good copy, and journalists covering it can cloak themselves in social responsibility—legitimately, up to a point; as a social issue, it merits coverage. But there is a fine line, easily crossed, between reporting and pushing. Few kids can hold out against what TV and magazines tell them everybody's doing.

"Dreading isolation, kids are increasingly unable to say, 'No,'" a school counselor tells the magazine. And isolation is never farther than a snub away. Parents are preoccupied, families withdrawn, communities rootless, friendship conditional. Is it any wonder children are drawn to sex? It may well seem to them the only relationship left. (MH)

"LOVE" CULT SNARES NAIVE STUDENTS

Shukan Post (November 1, 2002)

Don't look now, but there's a new religion in town. And college girls just love it. But, *Shukan Post* reports, stories have begun to trickle out that its purported path to salvation may be through sex with its founder.

The JMS Church derives its name from the initials of its Korean founder, Jong Myong Suk. Which, coincidentally—or perhaps not—are the same as "Jesus Morning Star," a reference to Revelations 2:24–29, in which Jesus promises believers, "He shall rule them with a rod of iron . . . and I will give him the morning star."

Jong, age 57, is said to have joined the Unification Church in his teens, but left to establish his own religion around 1980. It now claims 150,000 adherents in Korea and from the late 1980s also began making inroads in Japan, where it has attracted more than 1,000 members. Recruitment activities typically take place on college campuses, through infiltration of sports clubs and other extracurricular circles.

"The church's doctrine is composed of the so-called '30 precepts,' although it's pretty clear that they're derived from the Unification Church," explains Toyoshige Aizawa, a Christian minister engaged in weaning young people away from cults. "Jong has twisted the biblical story of Adam and Eve to deal with sex, saying, 'To atone for Adam and Eve's original sin, which was visited upon all mankind, it's necessary to engage in intercourse with the Lord.' In this case, he means himself, since he claims to be a reincarnation of Jesus."

In Korea, JMS is reportedly engaged in several legal battles regarding allegations of Jong's sexual hanky-panky, after a former adherent poured out her woes in a program aired on Korea's SBS TV in 1999.

Miss P, a Japanese woman who joined JMS in March 1997 while a student, relates her disillusionment with the "sex cult." "When sexual harassment accusations against Master Jong appeared on Internet bulletin boards, my superiors told me these were posted by people trying to justify their leaving the church by spreading lies," she tells *Shukan Post*.

In July 2000, Miss P was accorded the privilege of meeting the master in Osaka. She entered a carpeted room where she sat and was instructed to lie down facing upward. Then the master began administering a "health checkup," which she was told would "protect" her from women's ailments.

"He began feeling me up and poking me, saying '*Daijobu, daijobu* (It's all right).'" Afterward, an official said that the master had demonstrated his love for her, and swore her to secrecy.

About six months later, Miss P was summoned by the master once more. "This time he disrobed from the waist down and had sex with me," she claims. "It was no different from ordinary sex. And while he did it, he kept on repeating '*Daijobu, daijobu.*' It was then I realized my seniors and the other officials knew what was going on the whole time. That 'health checkup' was nothing but a blatant lie! I'll be paying for my naiveté for years to come."

This, perhaps, is where enlightenment really begins. (MS)

STAR ATHLETE IN GAY PORN FLICK

Shukan Gendai (November 9, 2002)

The pitcher is superstar material, no doubt about it. His record throughout his college career has been faultless, in terms of wins, strikeouts and earned-run average. He stands 180 cm (5 ft, 11 in) and can hurl a ball at 150 kph (93 mph). During this past season, he nearly single-handedly pulled his college team out of a slump.

There was no way the pro leagues were going to ignore a player of such extraordinary talent. In fact, three teams were interested in him, and he was expected to be a first-round draft choice this autumn. Conceivably, he could have gone on to become one of Japan's biggest baseball stars.

But that was before *Shukan Gendai* stumbled across something of career-ending proportions—a gay pornographic video in which the pitching ace is one of the stars. The video is fairly accessible and highly graphic in nature. The magazine managed to obtain a copy in a store specializing in homosexual pornography.

"It's being sold nationwide and has been promoted on the Internet. You can get hold of it quite easily, certainly through mail-order," says someone described in the article as being close to the gay pornographic industry. As for the content, it leaves little to the imagination. The baseball star's genitals are frequently visible, as the "mosaic," a video blurring effect, is used sparingly. His face is in full view during his 15-minute-long performance.

The film's story is of three college soccer players who accidentally slam into a car driven by some scary yakuza characters. As the young athletes try to apologize, the hoods force them to perform a series of humiliating acts of a sexual nature. In one raw scene, a hood clamps a collar around the baseball player's neck, forces him to his knees and brutally has his way with him.

Shukan Gendai declines to name either the player or his university. However, we are told the university is one of the nation's most prestigious when it comes to college baseball and that it's a member of the "big six" varsity baseball league, narrowing the list to the universities of Tokyo, Waseda, Keio, Rikkyo, Meiji and Hosei.

Armed with a photo taken from the video's jacket, the magazine approaches the coach of the ace's team. He denies knowledge of the video but confirms that the actor in the picture and his star pitcher are one and the same.

Although the video expert says that the player has long been open about his sexual orientation, the magazine's efforts to get in touch with the player are fruitless. Messages left on his answering machine get no response. When a reporter visits the university dormitory, the player is "out."

Meanwhile, the star's future appears to be in limbo. He is riding the bench while the university reviews whether he can be recruited by the pro leagues—if they still want him. (GB)

PORNO BIZ TARGETS PUBLIC BATHERS

Sunday Mainichi (July 27, 2003)

If you've visited a *sento*, a public bathhouse, in Tokyo lately, you've probably spotted this stern warning: "Bringing cell phones and other kinds of electronic devices here is prohibited as their use can cause trouble and misunderstanding among other customers."

The message is contained in a poster that has just been put up at about 1,000 sento and *onsen*, hot spring baths, throughout the capital. It stems from an incident last fall, according to one bathhouse operator. "There was a customer who was using a cell phone camera to record other customers while they were naked," the operator says.

It's clear that this incident is just the tip of a vast iceberg. *Sunday Mainichi* says the proliferation of camera-equipped cell phones, coupled with the continuously improved quality of the images they capture, have been a boon for Peeping Toms with a penchant for photography. "It seems they pretend to read their e-mail while actually they're taking pictures of the naked women," the bathhouse operator says.

This breed of photographer can easily get away with their illegal spying because they, too, are women, and thus their unsuspecting fellow female bathers let their guards down. But these snoops aren't hobbyists: Their aim is to sell their images and videos to the porn industry.

The market for such material is huge, and growing. Visit your local video retailer and in the porn corner you'll likely be confronted with a plethora of such titles as *Bathing in Broad Daylight*,

Snooping Heaven or *Toilet Trap*. An employee of one porn production company speculates that the genre accounts for around 10 percent of all pornographic titles on video and DVD.

While the portion may seem small, some simple calculations indicate that the market is worth billions of yen. Think about it: Shipments of all pornographic cassettes and discs total about 20 million units each year in Japan, with each product retailing in the order of several thousand yen. With so much money involved, it shouldn't be a surprise to learn that the covert photographers have become somewhat professional, both in their business acumen and photography skills.

"If we're talking about the price of purchased material, something that looks like it's going to sell really well will fetch ¥500,000 to ¥1 million" says a representative of a production company that specializes in hidden-camera pornography. "Just average stuff will go for ¥50,000 to ¥70,000."

The very best material is shot simultaneously with two or three devices by photographers who go to great lengths to get just the right angles. Yet it should also be pointed out that these dedicated professionals tend to break some serious laws in their pursuit of the perfect image or video.

"It's an invasion of our rights to privacy and constitutes illegal conduct," says Jiro Makino, a lawyer specializing in privacy and the Internet. "[A victim] can bring a damages suit against another person who collects information pertaining to where you are, who you are, and what kind of appearance you have." The covert photographers, he says, can also face such criminal charges as libel and blackmail. Yet it's doubtful whether the penalties will seriously deter the Peeping Toms.

An official of the Tokyo Metropolitan Police says, "With the proliferation of camera-equipped phones, we think that the number of cases is going to increase dramatically." (GB)

SENIORS FOUND IN NAUGHTY ROMP

Yomiuri Weekly (February 15, 2004)

Akiko, a nursing-home staffer in her 40s, has a problem with one of her patients, a man in his 80s: He exposes himself to her every morning. He is not senile; he just thinks he has something worth seeing. Nor is this unhealthy, says *Yomiuri Weekly*, however uncomfortable it makes Akiko. On the contrary, the man's pride and high spirits are heartening signs he remains attached to life.

What is the appropriate response? Should his liveliness be encouraged, or should he be administered a sharp warning to mind his manners?

The fact is, the magazine finds, the sex drive often remains active long past the stage in life where it can be indulged easily, conveniently and beautifully. Nursing homes are hotbeds of sexual feeling, if not of sex. But sometimes of sex as well, and it takes many forms. "Some female caregivers," confides the former director of a private nursing home, "help the male residents masturbate. Is this wise? I don't know. It's not real sex, of course, and frankly, as a man, I can understand how the men feel. I decided I wouldn't interfere."

"Sometimes," says a nurse, "a bedridden man will ejaculate when I wash his genitals. It's not as if he's chasing me for sex. And it gives him a feeling of confidence: 'Look! I'm still alive!' To me, it's just one aspect of care-giving."

Akiko and others have yet to attain that level of detachment. They admit to feelings of anger and revulsion. As professionals they struggle to cope, in the name of what some specialists call "sex rehabilitation."

That, though, is only part of the issue—the relatively easy part. A more serious problem, *Yomiuri Weekly* hears from those in the thick of it, is sex, love and marriage among the residents themselves. Marriage especially. That's a hornet's nest.

"We had this gentleman with us, a man in his late 80s," recalls a former nursing home staffer. "Upstanding fellow—military school graduate, company accountant until his retirement. His wife was dead. Anyway, we began finding ladies' underwear under his bed. We investigated, and found it belonged to a woman of 80 or so, whose room was connected by a veranda. To cut a long story short, she had been coming into his room at night . . ."

"Well, why not, if they love each other?" comments another former nursing home director. "So many men sink into apathy as they grow old. If a love affair lifts them out of that, so much the better."

Yes, but . . . marriage? Here the ambiguities multiply. It's not only the lovers who are involved but their money and their children, the latter tending to show teeth at the prospect of the former slipping through their filial fingers.

"If two residents fall in love and want to get married, their wishes should be respected," says a former home director—who adds, however, that it doesn't always work out that way in practice. It is generally the children who sign the contracts, and the children who pay the bills. And no nursing home wants its residents' children charging them with irresponsibility.

"One of our residents," the former director continues, "was a former corporate executive, very well off. A certain female caregiver would spend hours in his room. We questioned her: 'What's going on?' 'Nothing,' she insisted. But then they both left the home at the same time. It seems they got married, and when he died she came into a fortune. Luckily he had no children."

Within the next 10 years, the baby boom generation will start invading the nursing homes. That should be quite a party. (MH)

PARENTS SHOCKED BY SEX ED CONTENT

Shukan Shincho (March 25, 2004)

"Mom, do we have any condoms in the house? I need some for a school project. Oh, and by the way, how many times a week do you and dad have sex?"

The mother was speechless. Her own sex education hadn't prepared her for the sex education her son was receiving in his sixth-grade classroom.

Actually, reports *Shukan Shincho*, sex ed starts much earlier than grade six at Yokohama's Imajuku Public Elementary School. It starts in grade one. By grade three, the kids are writing reports that, says the magazine, are enough to make parents blush, if not faint. A brief sample: "The man's penis stiffens. He inserts it into the woman's vagina. When the man and woman are at the height of their excitement, the man secretes semen into the woman's body. The semen penetrates the woman's egg. And that is how life begins."

The technical term for this is "radical sex education." Imajuku Elementary initiated it in 1997, roused to drastic measures by a wave of bullying that had infected the school. Bullying, it was thought, stemmed from the children's failure to appreciate the sacredness of life. Perhaps if they understood how life is generated they would value it more.

Now at Imajuku, says *Shukan Shincho*, Life Studies is taught for 20 hours a year in grades one and two, 25 hours a year in grades three and four, and 30 hours a year in grades five and six. From first grade to graduation, students receive a total of 150 hours of Life Studies instruction—roughly 10 times the conventional concentration.

In grade one they learn basic terms like "penis" and "vagina." A booklet used as a supplementary text in grade three features detailed illustrations of various animals mating—insects, fish, snakes, dogs, cats, dolphins. The final chapter shows humans copulating. Interestingly enough, *Shukan Shincho* notes, the woman is on top.

What goes through a small child's mind as he or she takes all this in, asks the magazine? There is no easy way of knowing, and probably no way at all of generalizing. In any case, not all parents are pleased to have their children's precocity stoked so vigorously.

"You can teach this stuff to first-graders, but I doubt it means much," comments one parent. "All it does is arouse unnatural interest. At home, words like 'penis' and 'vagina' keep coming up. When a love scene appears on TV, the kids go, 'Is that intercourse?'"

A high-school teacher who observed an Imajuku grade-six sex education class had this to say: "It made me shudder a little to hear boys whose voices haven't even changed saying things like, 'When having sex you must keep your condom on from start to finish.' And little girls piping up, 'Rape is not mainly about sex, but about power.' It made me feel sad somehow."

A counter argument is that in a society in which sex is ubiquitous and inescapable and includes AIDS, rape, child pornography and teen pregnancy among its attributes, childhood innocence may be an unaffordable luxury. And in fact, *Shukan Shincho* says, radical sex education is spreading to other schools—though Imajuku itself is reportedly considering revising the program in response to some parents' objections.

The challenge is to calibrate sex education's quantity and content to what children can absorb. Professor emeritus Miyuki Ohashi of Tokyo Gakugei University thinks Imajuku Elementary lays it on a little thick. "Radical sex education is extremely dangerous," she says. "It teaches more than children need to know. What children see and hear they will soon want to try for themselves." (MH)

NEW GENERATION SAYS "NO" TO DOING IT

Yomiuri Weekly (October 31, 2004)

"Dear, shall we . . ." Akemi whispers shyly to her husband.

"No," he snaps. A moment later, ashamed of his brusqueness, he apologizes, pleading exhaustion from work and gently brushing his wife's tears from her cheeks. But nothing follows, and Akemi grimly faces a fact she had long been avoiding.

The word "sexless" entered the Japanese lexicon in 1994, and if "sexless marriage" seems an oxymoron, it describes all the same, says *Yomiuri Weekly*, a steadily expanding fact of Japanese life.

The Japan Sexology Society reports that in the late 1980s, roughly 10 percent of people seeking sexual counseling or therapy were in sexless marriages. Today that figure is close to 40 percent. And the couples in question are getting younger. Some 60 percent of sexless couples seen by the society's counselors are in their 30s; 20 percent are in their 20s. Akemi is 34, her husband 36.

In 80 percent of cases, the direct cause is traceable to the husband. "What's wrong with young husbands today?" asks *Yomiuri Weekly*.

One interesting hypothesis comes from Shoko Ieda, a nonfiction writer who has researched the problem. "Nowadays," she says, "thanks to cosmetics and beauty treatment clinics, all women are reasonably good-looking, very few outstandingly so. Men no longer set their sights on one particular woman—'I've just got to get that girl.' A sexual conquest no longer brings with it a special sense of accomplishment." Result: chronically diminished desire.

Teruo Abe, director of a mental health clinic, notes the tendency of marriage to reduce the man-woman relationship to something more like the relationship between mother and child, or brother and sister. You continue to like each other and depend on each other—but sex? It seems almost incestuous.

Mr. T, 43, has an unusual sideline. An unassuming salaryman by day, come evening he is one of a corps of "sexual volunteers," "servicing" wives in sexless marriages. The corps is run by sex counselor Kim Myung Gun, who says, "Men have *fuzoku*"—commercial ero-entertainment in all its glittering variety. But there's nothing like that for women. So I thought, why not introduce troubled women to men who would enjoy ministering to them?"

Volunteer applicants, he says, are rigorously screened. And the transaction is not commercial—no money changes hands.

"After this interview," Mr. T tells *Yomiuri Weekly*'s reporter, "I'm meeting two women—one for dinner, the other probably to go to a hotel." In the year and a half he's been at this, he has "serviced" nearly 30 women—two-thirds of them housewives in their 40s.

Between 30 and 50 women a month are "serviced" by Kim's volunteers. The women range in age from 20 to over 50. Many have been sexless for about 10 years, some for as long as 20. More than a few of them, says Mr. T, break down in tears of gratitude. "They feel they've at last been given their due as women.

"I wonder," he adds, "if their husbands understand what they're going through."

"What about your marriage?" inquires *Yomiuri Weekly*.

"Sexless for years," he replies.

Are men and women really made for each other? "For a woman," observes sex counselor Kim, "marriage is a beginning. For a lot of men, it's the goal. Once a child is born, the husband has his blueprint family, which in many cases is all he wanted. From then on, conjugal life for him is more or less superfluous." (MH)

EX FIRST LADY IN SEX SCANDAL?

Shukan Taishu (February 14, 2005)

Lurid photos of a woman said to be a former prime minister's wife in the throes of ecstasy while being suckled by a young political secretary could destroy global trust in Japan, according to *Shukan Taishu*.

A blurred snapshot of the naked couple was apparently taken during one of the numerous bi-weekly sessions the woman arranged with the young man in a Shinjuku hotel while her husband was busy looking after Japan's concerns.

"Their faces are covered with a mosaic and it's hard to tell who the woman really is," a Diet member's political secretary says. An accompanying story says the husband was prime minister at some time since the 80s. There have been 10 prime ministers from Noboru Takeshita to Yoshiro Mori. The woman was also described as having been a 'fairly active and attractive first lady,' which narrows the choices down to about four in 10. Some places have printed the name of the prime minister, while others have given lists of just a few names. "All the talk in (the political district of) Nagatacho is about which former prime minister's wife it could be," says the secretary.

Disclosure of the photo now could have something to do with the political ambitions of the man in the photo. "The guy with the woman is said to have been a secretary for the prime minister, but has since successfully run for office in a local government election. Now, he's supposed to be aiming for the House of Representatives," a political insider says. "Somebody's probably trying to get him involved in a scandal to keep him from getting a place in the Diet."

If the lowbrow men's weekly is correct, the man in the photo has no one to blame but himself for the snapshot becoming public. It says the man is supposed to have showed a friend, another political secretary, the photos of a steamy session with the woman he claimed was a one-time prime minister's wife.

Photos developed in Japan traditionally come with an index of thumbnail shots so that every photo in an entire film can be viewed at a single glance. The friend cut the thumbnail of the photo currently being sent around and showed it to his girlfriend. It was too small for her to make out the details, so she took it to a nearby convenience store photocopier to blow it up. It's the expanded copy of the picture that has gone public.

"The girlfriend was in a hurry when she did the photocopying and left the original shot on the photocopier. Nobody's got a clue what happened to the original," a political source tells *Shukan Taishu*. "The friend says there were about 10 photos in all. Three were of the nude man and woman probably taken by a camera using a self-timer. The first one has the secretary sucking on the woman's breasts and a second shot seems to be a little later while the guy has turned his attentions to licking the woman's neck. He can't remember the details of the third shot. He did say the remaining seven shots were all of the woman in raunchy poses." (RC)

USED BOXERS FIND NEW MARKET

Shukan Jitsuwa (June 28, 2001)

"Originally our store targeted male customers; we never thought women would come to shop," the salesclerk tells *Shukan Jitsuwa*. "But these days, we're getting more gals all the time."

The store, located in an unnamed city in northeast Japan, is known as a *burusera*, a specialized type of outlet that appeals to male collectors with a fetish for the bloomers, panties and middie blouses of high school girls. Used articles are supposedly supplied to such stores by the girls themselves, and certain esoteric items have been known to command hefty prices.

The shop recently diversified its traditional product selection to include used men's briefs, school uniforms, socks and other articles. For which women, as incredible as it may seem, are willing to lay out their hard-earned money to acquire.

Several years back, men's briefs made a splash, so to speak, when certain squeamish housewives confided to the media that so begrimed were their husbands shorts, they shrank from handling them, using chopsticks to drop them into the wash. Sensing a business opportunity, an appliance manufacturer even marketed a two-vat washing machine so dad's grimy shorts could be isolated from the rest of the family wash.

Now, it seems, women are buying these garments to heighten their passion while practicing *hitori etchi,* as solitary sex is referred to here. *Shukan Jitsuwa* proceeds to Netherland, an "adult shop" situated in Shinjuku's sleazy Kabukicho district, where the manager acknowledges that a market for such goods has existed for several years.

As in the case with feminine goods, items that have been worn for extended periods without laundering and those that retain certain, er, discharges are said to command a higher price. Another source of titillation for females appears to be items popular with gay men. One woman admits she enjoys logging on to gay sites on the Web and ogling pics of teenage rock performers and other cute guys in action.

Hirano, who manages a shop named Cabarie in the Shinjuku 2-chome district, a familiar gay hangout, says most of the women who shop in his store are in their 20s. "They don't seem to be students or bar types. I don't really know how to describe most of them . . ."

"You can find outfits selling men's used underwear on the Internet," says a 27-year-old customer who gave the name Yuka. "I went ahead and bought one.

"Why? I guess I have a fetish for scents," she giggles. "If I smell a sexual odor, I get incredibly turned on—it's much more realistic than looking at a movie or still photo. Now I understand what it's like for men who buy girls' items in burusera shops."

To enhance the sensation obtained from ownership of these musty treasures, the Internet sites offering such items invariably provide data concerning the brief's former owner, often including full frontal nude photos and a profile that lists his height, weight and occupation.

Take it one step further, and you've got a matchmaking service that conforms to the laws concerning truth in packaging. (MS)

TRADITION WANES; STRIP CLUBS SAG

Shukan Shincho (July 12, 2001)

It's a rainy Saturday night at the Asakusa Rock-za, one of the country's best-known strip clubs, and only about an eighth of the seats are filled. Four women wearing hot pants and tank tops take to the stage where they dance in the style of teenage idols. Eventually one remains. She lets down her long hair. Momentarily, the only thing she has on is an anklet. The act ends with our starlet lifting one leg high in the air, struggling to maintain the pose.

Shukan Shincho's reporter leaves the show in a gloomy mood. After examining the offerings at this and a number of other major strip clubs around the country, the magazine concludes that the sun is indeed setting on what used to be Japan's premier form of adult entertainment.

Hiroo Minowa, the author of a book chronicling the postwar history of strip shows in Japan, agrees. "I think the peak was around the mid-80s," he says. "The number of strip theaters around Japan was about 250, and they weren't limited to the busy areas of Shinjuku, Asakusa or Ikebukuro. They were also located at hot spring resorts and in small huts."

Minowa puts the current number of theaters at no more than 120. Similarly, the number of dancers has shrunk from around 2,000 to no more than 800. He blames the decline on the recession and more stringent laws.

The modern Japanese strip show traces its roots to 1947. That's when the Teito-za Theater in Shinjuku introduced "picture-frame shows," in which topless young women posed inside picture frames.

The shows were a gimmick to attract theater customers during the grim economic times. Soon a slew of other theaters got in on the act, and the models went from topless to full-on nude.

During the next couple of decades, strip shows flourished, as theaters popped up throughout the country and the size of audiences ballooned. But the Mideast oil embargo of 1973 plunged the country into chaos as people hoarded goods and cut back on entertainment expenses.

"The customers stopped coming," says Minowa. "So the shows started offering live sex acts and bestiality. . . . From around 1975, there wasn't anything they wouldn't show."

Yet the biggest shock came in the mid-80s, with the strengthening of a law regulating nightlife entertainment. "Operating after hours was outlawed," says Minowa, "and theaters gradually started going out of business."

The change also coincided with the introduction of new types of sexual services, and the proliferation of pornographic videos and porn via the Internet hasn't exactly helped.

In short, it's no longer a novelty to see beautiful women naked. The Japanese strip show, concludes *Shukan Shincho*, is quickly becoming a relic from the past. (GB)

FOREIGNERS LURED BY COFFEE AND SWAPPING

Shukan Jitsuwa (November 22, 2001)

When romantic couples are out on the town and in the mood for a bit of hanky-panky, they often head to *"kappuru kissa"* (lit. couples' coffee shop). The advantages these sex lounges have over other such places, notably love hotels, is that adventurous types can easily swap partners with other customers, who are often total strangers. This attraction hasn't been lost on a growing number of foreigners in Japan, according to *Shukan Jitsuwa*.

An unnamed Kansai writer with a research interest in the local sex industry explains: "The kapuru kissa in [the Osaka districts of] Umeda and Shinsaibashi are getting several foreign couples each week. It seems they started coming after checking out the Internet."

To find out more, the magazine stops off in Osaka, home to about 40 such establishments.

At Dang Erous in Umeda, the owner confirms a surge of foreign interest in his establishment. "There are Germans, Italians, Moroccans and so on. Even at this moment, on a Monday, there are several here."

The foreign customers at Dang Erous tend to be serious, hard-working types who, it seems, are out to release some tension. The women are usually in their 20s, with around 40 percent of them university students. The men are generally in their 30s and work at foreign language schools.

Next, our reporter heads to Tokyo to investigate Sea Dash in Shinjuku. There, he encounters a blond American couple. He is 32, hails from Kansas and works for a securities firm. She is a secretary for a foreign oil company in Tokyo. Our reporter—whose curiosity at this point seems to have strayed beyond the boundaries of professionalism—can't help noticing that she also has a compact, well-proportioned body.

He learns that the couple patronizes kapuru kissa about three or four times a month, including ones in Roppongi and Shibuya. "I usually have around two or three people [per visit], while she gets around five. The sex is fun," the guy says.

Within no time, the three of them, along with the reporter's date, retire to Sea Dash's "playroom," a space illuminated with black light and, on this night, containing about half a dozen couples in various forms of embrace.

At Milky House, in Nagoya, the most common nationalities among the foreign clientele are Korean and Chinese, although the majority of them arrive with Japanese partners. The shop's owner says Japanese customers are at first often perplexed and uncomfortable at the sight of foreign customers. But once the action starts, "it seems nationality no longer matters," he says. "Lechery knows no borders."

An interesting aspect of these couplings is the reaction of Japanese women, the magazine notes. When they first team up with foreign men, it is the latter who take the lead. But once the action gets going, the women tend to become the aggressors.

One female Japanese customer seems to take her role in these foreign affairs very seriously indeed. "For world peace, it's important to start by putting naked skin against naked skin," she says. (GB)

UGLY WOMEN DRAW MEN LIKE FLIES

Shukan Taishu (December 24, 2001)

It's a nightmare that any hard-drinking reader of *Shukan Taishu* can relate to. A drinking buddy urges you on to one more place, a hostess bar where, you are assured, "the women are gorgeous." But as you enter, something seems amiss. Then, once your vision has adapted to the darkness, it hits you—the hostesses are anything but gorgeous. In fact, they are hideous. Maybe they are old enough to be your mother, or are the size of sumo wrestlers. Or perhaps they aren't even women at all.

If so, you have entered a *getekyaba*. And now that the pre-New Year drinking season is upon us, the magazine warns, some of us may find ourselves inadvertently trapped inside one.

"*Kyaba*" means cabaret. For "*gete*," however, there is no equivalent word in English. Think of something both weird and sleazy but conducted with gusto. These clubs cater to some of the strangest proclivities known to humankind.

One of the first places in Tokyo that our intrepid magazine reporter checks out is a bar in western Tokyo boasting of its jumbo-size female staff. His first sight of the enormous girth of his hostess leaves him slack-jawed.

She squeezes in beside him on an inordinately tiny sofa. Her business card is pink and advertises her weight: 140 kg (309 lbs). "At this club, if you weigh less than 90 kg (198 lbs), you get fired," she boasts. "This isn't like other establishments. The bigger you are, the better." The reporter certainly doesn't understand the physical appeal of these places. Yet he immensely enjoys the conversation.

"Many of the customers here are in their 30s," says Miss L, who weighs in at 105 kg (231 lbs). "Everyone has their favorite body region. The flesh around the stomach, or tree-trunk thighs . . . But I guess what many of these guys have in common is a mother complex."

Next on the itinerary is Ikebukuro, the location of a club whose hostesses could not exactly be described as young and attractive. "There are people for whom only ugly women will do," says one of the middle-aged and homely women working there. In that sense, some guys even have pretty high standards. "Recently, we have been getting guys who come in and complain, 'What's going on? This is just like any other place.'"

The reporter rounds out his odyssey in Shinjuku's Kabukicho. At one establishment, he is greeted by a hostess wearing a slinky black dress and fishnet stockings. But this "hostess" also happens to have a gravelly voice and the build of a rugby player, and appears to be in the early stages of growing a beard. He explains that his bar serves as a kind of rest and relaxation spot for women who work in bars and nightclubs.

"We entertain them, and then later they will cater to us. We also get hostesses who bring their regular customers. While we get friendly with them, the women can have a break," he says.

By this point, our reporter's assignment is over. Although he took it on with a distinct sense of trepidation, he has actually ended up enjoying himself. Men might want to heed his advice this drinking season—if you find yourself bored of being constantly surrounded by beautiful hostesses, there is always the getekyaba. (GB)

ANCIENT SEX CUSTOM REVIVED

Shukan Jitsuwa (December 27, 2001)

In the West, when a man approaches a woman on his hands and knees, it's usually to offer an abject apology for some real or imagined slight. In Japan, however, approaching a lady on all fours is more likely to evoke memories of a long-extinct sexual custom known as *yobai*, literally "night crawling."

Kenkyusha's dictionary defines the term thus: "to steal into a house to see a woman under cover of night."

Sneaking into a lady's boudoir was a custom dating back to remote antiquity. But following the introduction of incandescent lighting and doors with locks, the practice had—except for a few determined holdouts—begun to die out by the late 19th century.

These days, however, entrepreneurs are reviving yobai as a commercial form of titillation, reports *Shukan Jitsuwa*. In addition to adult videos featuring yobai, for instance, aspiring practitioners can now go down on all fours and creep toward the girl of their dreams in computer games. While for those who insist on something more realistic, "image clubs"—establishments that invite customers to act out their favorite fantasies—now offer "yobai play."

"The way it works at our shop, the customer peeps into the room from outside the door and watches the girl fondling herself in bed," explains the operator of an establishment in Tokyo's Ikebukuro district. "Then after what is made to look like an unsatisfactory session, she puts a mask over her eyes and pretends to fall asleep." That's the cue for the customer to come crawling in. "I don't know how yobai works at competitors' places, but lately it's been really popular with our customers," he adds.

Yobai has also boomed as a theme in adult videos. A video production agency called Wild Side has been producing its *Night Crawlers* series since 1999. Its latest is titled *Yobai No. 15.*

"Actually we started it with the idea of producing a genre that no one else was offering and never expected it to do that well," Wild Side's PR rep tells the magazine. "But customer numbers grew and the series became our second most popular after *Chijo (Female Pervert)*. Unfortunately, hardly any customers mail back the response card, so we're not really sure what's motivating their purchases."

Yobai No. 15 contains an omnibus of five fanciful scenarios. In *I'd Like to Get Back at That Hoity-toity Girl Next Door*, a young woman is shown shopping at a convenience store. The camera follows her home, lens positioned as if a stalker were observing her. She enters her apartment, undresses and prepares for slumber.

The "crawler" then enters. The romantic scene that follows, illuminated solely by a flashlight, shows the two coupling while the female "sleeps" on, enjoying herself as if engaged in an erotic dream and apparently remaining asleep.

The four other scenarios are titled *A Working Girl in a Dormitory*; *Finding a Hotel Room With the Door Left Unlocked*; and *She Got Blind Drunk at a Party and Let her Guard Down.*

"These days, depictions of sex are everywhere," explains an authority on adult videos. "People are tired of the same old stuff. They find yobai exciting for its sheer depravity. Since men today have such meek personalities, they're not titillated by the idea of violent rape; rather, they are turned on by the idea of sneaking into a darkened room . . ."

But might not these vicarious experiences prompt someone to take up night crawling for real? After all, concludes *Shukan Jitsuwa* with a sigh, old customs may appear to die out, but men's tastes don't change that easily. (MS)

LUXURY SEX LURES HIGH ROLLERS

Shukan Jitsuwa (January 10–17, 2002)

For businesses everywhere, there is no escaping the economy's deflationary spiral. Consumers are stingier than ever, and on the rare occasions when they do take out their pocketbooks, they expect rock-bottom prices. The sex industry is no different. The past few years have seen prices at massage parlors drop from ¥10,000 to less than ¥4,000.

Yet, at the same time, *Shukan Jitsuwa* notes, a counter-trend has also emerged in the sex industry involving exclusive and high-priced services. The magazine zeroes in on an outfit called *Ishiki no Tobira* ("Door of Consciousness"), located in Tokyo's Nakano Ward. Its "courses" run as high as ¥300,000—and that doesn't include sexual intercourse.

Who can afford such luxury in these days of economic peril? The owner of Ishiki no Tobira answers that the changing economy, while throwing record numbers of people out of work and slashing overall personal incomes, has also spawned a small class of super-wealthy men. "Yet, despite that, only discount sex establishments are being set up, while we haven't seen any exclusive places to cater to these VIP-class guys," he says.

The establishment is strictly members only. The owner, whose name is not given, screens applicants, nearly all of whom are professionals. Likewise, for every 30 women interviewed, only one or two are accepted. "It's simply not enough for them to look good. I select the ones who also seem to sparkle," he says. "We aim not only to provide sensual pleasure but also to give spiritual comfort."

The ¥300,000 course provides just that for four hedonistic hours, but the reporter's expense account, alas, rules that out. Instead, he opts for the ¥100,000 service that lasts one hour and 40 minutes—or ¥1000 per minute. At the appointed time and place, our reporter is met by a chauffeur-driven Mercedes-Benz. Inside is Anna, who is 23 and wearing an elegant dress. She introduces herself, and already our reporter's spirit is starting to feel a bit of that comfort the owner was talking about.

The car arrives at a five-star hotel, where the reservation has already been taken care of. Upon entering the room, the reporter is pleasantly surprised to find another woman, Ryoko, waiting there. In contrast to svelte Anna, the 19-year-old appears more of a girl-next-door type.

One of the women pours his drinks and as he gazes out at the night skyline of Tokyo, the *Shukan Jitsuwa* reporter is starting to feel like a true master of the universe. He is bathed and massaged. Then comes the main event, a bout of three-way frolicking on the bed. Afterward, the girls apply a facial pack and give our hardworking journalist another massage, but this time a serious one involving a medicated lotion.

Ishiki no Tobira's owner says, "We have some regular customers who take the ¥300,000 course a couple of times a week. We even had one offer ¥1.8 million to have a girl for 24 hours." It's clearly a service that Ishiki no Tobira's clients can't get enough of—at any price. (GB)

FULL-TIME JOB FOR PICK-UP ARTISTS

Shukan Taishu (April 22, 2002)

Ah, to be a "scoutman" in Shibuya in spring!

In March and April, Tokyo is awash in fresh faces from the countryside—newcomers starting school, starting jobs, starting a new life generally. Just possibly a scout may latch onto a girl who hasn't heard his pitch before, and who isn't too sophisticated to disdain it.

It's an anonymous profession, and *Shukan Taishu* identifies its sources only as Mr. A and Mr. Y. They are freelancers, selling their services to *kyabakura*, "health clubs" and other catchily named establishments of the recreational sex trade. From his base of operations at Shibuya Station's famed Hachiko statue, Mr. A accosts 300 to 400 young women a day. So thick are the crowds, so restricted is a person's movement, so impossible is it to dart down the block after a likely prospect, that he is reduced to pitching his spiel to whoever happens to press close to him.

For that very reason, Mr. Y shuns Shibuya, preferring less fashionable venues like Ueno and Shinagawa. The uphill nature of the pursuit doesn't dampen his enthusiasm. "For every 10,000 girls I approach," he says, "100 give me a cell phone number. Of those, maybe 30 actually show up at the establishment for an interview. Of the 30, 15 are hired. And of those 15, three stay more than a month."

Does the scout care how long they stay? That depends on the system under which he draws his pay. There are two. The first, the lump-sum system, accords him a flat fee from the club for every girl he introduces. Under the second, he draws 5 to 10 percent of the girl's daily earnings. "That's great," says Mr. Y, "if all goes well. Money rains down on you while you sleep. Trouble is, girls these days quit over the least little dissatisfaction, and if they stay less than a month, the scout loses."

It's a job like any other, with its good points and its bad. A scout must face the fact, characteristic of many walks of life—and of life itself –that the easiest marks bring the lowest returns.

Who are the easiest marks? "Girls whose style of dress is two or three months behind the times," says Mr. Y. Smarter-looking girls are more resistant. Conquering that resistance must be the aim of every scout, for fees under the lump-sum system vary from ¥20,000 to ¥200,000, and the girl's attractiveness is the measure. "I'll let you in on a little secret," says Mr. A. "The best-selling girls at the moment are those with black hair and white skin—the quiet types."

You might suppose a scout's work is done once he has shepherded a prospect to a club. Not so. There is "after-care" to see to. "My cell phone is on 24 hours a day," sighs Mr. Y, "and any complaint from one of my girls, however trivial, must be listened to." (MH)

HOSTS SERVICE FEMALE PATRONS

Tsukuru (June, 2002)

In 1966, a suave 36-year-old entrepreneur named Takeshi Aida figured that if millions of men paid money to drink in the company of attractive hostesses, an establishment in which the gender roles were reversed might make it as well. Aida proceeded to launch Night Tokyo, Japan's first host club, near Tokyo Station. For the past 25 years, his flagship club, Ai, has been a landmark across town in the Kabukicho entertainment district, securing Aida's reputation as Japan's "King of Hosts."

Writing in the monthly *Tsukuru* magazine, Akira Hinago reports that about two years ago, the number of host clubs in Kabukicho alone had soared to around 100, leading to many troubles. "I'd rather you didn't call those places 'host clubs,'" sniffs Aida. "More than half are pubs without a license. The reason they became popular was they appealed to customers who like pubs."

The degree to which the trade has deteriorated is borne out by the recent death of a 20-year-old Kabukicho club host. His colleagues, overhearing him fib that he had played at the National High School Baseball Tournament, decided to teach him a lesson. Beaten repeatedly over a period of 10 days, he succumbed to his injuries in early April; police subsequently arrested 15 hosts at his club on manslaughter and related charges. In a separate incident in Nagoya on March 29, a host whose attitude irritated his peers was fatally lynched on his first day of work.

Both victims were employed at the newer variety of pub-style host clubs. These establishments are typically patronized by unattached young women working in massage parlors or cabarets who seek relief after a hard day's night. "There's really no place to go after work," complains a 21-year-old cabaret hostess, who visits such clubs twice weekly. "If we're caught dating customers we're dismissed. That's because if we have sex with them on the outside, they'll stop patronizing the shop."

The newer clubs typically sublease the premises of other bars after closing time, paying rents far below the going rate. This enables them to charge customers the comparatively low rate of ¥15,000 to ¥20,000 per visit. The hosts are easily recruited from the ranks of students and part-timers.

As more clubs opened, competition intensified, leading management to send its young hosts to hustle for business out on the street. Even junior high school girls were enticed to enter, served a glass of oolong tea, and then presented with a bill for ¥20,000. If they couldn't pay, the club would demand payment from their parents.

Local gangsters, who consider the sidewalks their own turf, began roughing up the hosts and proceeded to squeeze more club operators for protection money. "There's a glut on the market now," sighs a female host-club operator. "Things went fine when times were good; but when things got rough, hosts formed cliques or fought over women. They can be worse than yakuza.

"I'd say these places are on the way out."

Hosts, moreover, have been disappointed to learn the job isn't exactly a piece of cake. Some have even been treated, well, like sex objects. "Just going there to drink won't satisfy me," pouts one customer. "I expect the host to take me to a hotel. Or else I take my business elsewhere. They've all got a quota to fill, so they'll do it."

Since hosts are expected to foot the bill for the hotel and for any meals consumed during the encounter, they often pay out roughly the same amount it costs their customer to visit the club.

The wages of sin are low indeed. (MS)

NEW BIZ HIDES WORKERS' LURID PASTS

Shukan Taishu (September 23, 2002)

When the time came for Rika, 28, to tie the knot and settle down, she encountered an unexpected dilemma. She'd spent the past several years working as a masseuse in the "pink" industry. And—all the more cause for this bride to blush pink—she'd met her fiance on the job.

The problem was, Mr. Right came from an old-fashioned family that insisted on nothing less than a big wedding. Which meant attendance by both the groom's and bride's extended families would be obligatory.

But Rika had severed ties with her family years ago. What to do? Well, for a not-inconsiderable sum, Rika arranged for a professional *aribai-ya*, or alibi service, to subcontract a small agency that specializes in booking professional actors. The agency supplied her "parents" and a dozen or so family members to attend the affair, and no one was the wiser.

"At the banquet, the man who played the role of my father delivered a great speech," Rika giggles. "He moved my hubby's parents to tears."

These aribai-ya, according to *Shukan Taishu*, began springing up about 20 years ago. Their first customers were married women, who turned to them as a last resort to help cover up illicit love affairs. From there, the clientele shifted mostly to women employed in the pink trade, who are currently believed to feed 80 to 90 percent of the business.

"Magazines that recruit women for these jobs are full of ads that promise 'Full alibi services available, so you can work without concern,'" notes a 32-year-old man employed by one such outfit. "I guess you can pretty much say it's a case of one hand washing the other."

Some of these acts of deception, however, stem from genuine necessity. Take Nana, 21, who moved to Tokyo from Nagano last April and took up employment at an "image club" in Ikebukuro. "I was nearly broke when I got to Tokyo, so I was sleeping overnight in the shop," she relates. "After a while I'd saved up enough money to rent my own pad. But I had an awful time finding a broker that would rent to me."

Realtors and landlords, it seems, tend to shun the patronage of women in the pink business, perhaps fearing they might use the premises to bring home customers for wild sexual liaisons that would downgrade property values.

For assistance, Nana turned to an aribai-ya, who, for a set amount, fixed her up with credentials identifying her as an employee in a company that markets imported goods. She was issued a counterfeit employee ID tag and a tax withholding certificate, enough to convince the realtor that she was a perfectly respectable office worker.

That's not to say these transactions always go smoothly. When another girl, Sachiko, 22, needed a guarantor for her apartment lease, the man clearly let her know he was willing to put pleasure before business. "He told me if I went to bed with him, he'd draw up the documents I needed for free," she huffs to *Shukan Taishu*. "How tacky can you get?!" (MS)

SEX BIZ HEALTHY DESPITE RECESSION

dacapo (May 21, 2003)

Maybe we should let the sex industry run Japan?

Just think, muses *dacapo*. The sex industry represents everything the government has promised for years to accomplish for the nation as a whole. Here, "structural reform" is an ongoing fact, not an empty slogan. "Decentralization," "deregulation," "internationalization"—the words are familiar, but to see them at work we must turn not to national affairs, but to the commercial sex trade.

The results are heartening to all proponents of reform. The vigor of the sex business is in startling contrast to the torpor elsewhere in the economy. In 2001 sexual transactions nationwide were valued at ¥2.3 trillion. Young women unable to land jobs elsewhere know there's a place for them here. Entrepreneurs find, in this sector as in no other, outlets for their energy and creativity.

What is the secret behind this relentless recession-defying expansion? "One point," the magazine hears from an analyst, "is that it's a business rooted in human instincts, so demand is assured whatever the state of the economy.

"More important though," he continues, "is the dynamism, the endless innovation. There's no country in the world that offers the variety of sexual services Japan does." He cites the latest novelties: young girls removing their panties and selling them on the spot; "reverse pick-up establishments" where girls go to pick up paying guys. "It's a field that's constantly breeding new ideas."

It's been doing that for a long time. A spirit rooted in the premodern licensed pleasure quarters re-emerged in the "salons" of the

1950s, where amateur hostesses gradually expanded their repertoire from social chit-chat over drinks to "sexy services" after them.

In the late 1970s came the *no-pan kissa*, coffee shops featuring mini-skirted pantyless waitresses striding across mirrored floors. The mid-'90s gave us "image clubs," where the socially unacceptable impulse reigns supreme and you can be the man you always wanted to be: a teacher with a pliant schoolgirl, a patient with a willing nurse, an uncouth groper in the subway of least resistance—and so on.

Here internationalization thrives, and connoisseurs know where to go for whatever a passing mood calls for: Russian dancers in Akasaka, Colombian strippers in Roppongi, Thai, Chinese, Korean and Filipina aestheticians here, there and just about everywhere.

But what really gave the industry the jolt to which it throbs to this day, says *dacapo*, was the *deriheru* innovation of 1999. Deriheru means "delivery health." "Health" means sex. If she goes to your place, its not prostitution; the law has nothing to say about it.

Koichiro Nakamura, 34, was running a construction company back in 1999, and losing his shirt. Then a three-line deriheru newspaper ad caught his eye. Just for fun he published an ad of his own, with his phone number. The phone rang and rang. Well, there was his answer. He scouted a girl on the street, installed a separate phone line, and he was in business. His wife wasn't pleased at first, but "that first month I made close to ¥2 million." He ditched the construction company and went into deriheru full-time.

Chiaki, 20, went job-hunting after high school and drew a blank. That's not unusual. In 2002, *dacapo* says, only 56 percent of junior college grads found jobs. What's a girl to do? "I had to earn a living," says Chiaki. At a Shibuya "loveland" she nets ¥500,000 a month. She works five days a week, 4 P.M. to 11 P.M. "I never dreamed it would be this busy," she says. That's the way it is with a business "rooted in human instincts." (MH)

HOT BARS FEATURE THE LIVE ACT

Shukan Post (April 16, 2004)

Inside a "play room," three guys are getting acquainted with a young woman dressed in a nurse's costume. Yet in a few minutes, the costume will become immaterial after the guys remove it and then engage in a naked orgy with the lone woman.

Meanwhile, outside the play room's walls, a large scrum of voyeurs is keenly observing the steamy events as they unfold—the "walls" are really one-way mirrors.

Two reporters from *Shukan Post*, a man and a woman, are in the crowd, here to investigate the most talked-about trend in the sex business—"happening bars."

Happening bars are where sex, quite literally, happens among the customers. They recently came into the public spotlight after porn actor Chocoball Mukai was arrested for indecent exposure for his alleged performance in one such establishment.

They first appeared on the scene in 1999. According to Toru Kihara, a journalist specializing in the sex industry, the first few establishments were gathering spots for swingers. Then about a year or two ago, their number began skyrocketing. Today there are about 100 of them, 30 in Tokyo alone, Kihara reckons.

The magazine's reporters managed to enter a bar in the Kabuki-cho district of Tokyo's Shinjuku Ward, the scene of the play room antics described above. The first thing the intrepid reporters encountered was strict security. The door to the establishment was locked and entrance was gained after speaking through an intercom. The woman was asked her name. The man, however, was also required to provide his age, address and telephone number. He was also asked to show ID.

It was the same arrangement at another happening bar in the Roppongi district of Tokyo. "We have a system that refuses entry to questionable people, so that everyone here can feel at ease," the bar's owner says.

The point is taken once the reporters notice who "everyone" consists of –people from respectable, extremely conventional walks of life. "All the customers are very ordinary office ladies, civil servants or the like," the bar's owner says. "We also get what you might call 'elite women,' as well as salarymen working at large corporations, government officials, doctors and lawyers."

Among the "elite women" is a doctor working in the orthopedic surgery department of a public hospital. "I feel I can let loose here, since it's a bar," she tells the reporters. "You can forget about your work while you're in such an unreal kind of place."

That lots of men would patronize such bars doesn't surprise *Shukan Post*. But why do they attract so many women, particularly ones who otherwise lead such ordinary lives?

"[The women have] a strong desire to transform themselves, to give themselves a new "face" that is different from the face they wear every day," explains psychologist Akitsugu Kuwasaki. "The secret of the happening bars' popularity is the sense of security they provide. They are strictly managed and don't allow information leaks."

That, says Kuwasaki, allows the women to lead a straitlaced existence by day, while by night they can indulge in their wildest fantasies. (GB)

SEXY DOLLS SEDUCE OWNERS

dacapo (April 21, 2004)

"The other day, we took a drive out to Mount Fuji," reads the letter. "I've enclosed some photos from our trip. Take care of your health, because the weather's gotten colder."

Along with the warm handwritten note, signed "Yoshiko," were several photos of a fetching female, some alone, some posed with a man who appeared to be in his 30s, obviously her boyfriend.

The letter's recipient was Hideo Tsuchiya, president of Orient Industry Co. and Yoshiko's "father," so to speak. Tsuchiya specializes in the design and manufacture of life-size mannequins which—with no disrespect intended to citizens of the Netherlands—are referred to in Japan as "Dutch wives." The dolls serve as sex substitutes for widowers, the handicapped and other males who are able to function sexually but who, for whatever reason, lack human partners.

Presumably, the gentleman in the photos penned the note to express his satisfaction with the relationship.

"I often get letters like this one," Tsuchiya tells *dacapo*. "It's gratifying. But you know, a Dutch wife is not merely a doll, or an object. She can be an irreplaceable lover, who provides a sense of emotional healing."

Speaking at his showroom near JR Okachimachi Station, where some two dozen of the ersatz females are displayed, Tsuchiya tells the reporter that for years his clientele had typically been handicapped men, or single men over 40. But about six years ago, when he commenced sales via the Internet, he was mildly surprised to receive a surge of orders from men in their 20s and 30s.

The showroom models are dressed (or undressed) to kill, some clad in designer fashions and wearing Bulgari wristwatches, others in flimsy negligees. The latest best seller, named "Jewel," went on sale three years ago, after two years in development. Jewel stands 140 cm (4 ft, 7 in.) tall and weighs 26 kg (57 lbs), and no seams are visible where the limbs or head join the torso.

"Please, go ahead, touch her," Tsuchiya urges. "Instead of vinyl, we use high-grade silicon, which gives a texture close to human skin. The feeling is completely different from the inflatable type." Perfecting the process required considerable investment in equipment but has paid off, as Orient Industry has already sold about 600 dolls, despite Jewel's hefty price tag of ¥600,000. "We've made the body more pliant, and the legs will open wider," says Tsuchiya.

"Isn't she cute?" he beams, eyes twinkling with obvious pride.

dacapo's reporter confesses: "When I ran my hand along the doll's thigh, I felt a shiver of excitement."

After observing the painstaking effort that goes into the making of each doll, the reporter came away enlightened. "Many people might be inclined to disparage sex toys," he writes, "but these dolls truly exemplify Japan's status as a high-tech country!"

Jewel and her sisters are shipped to purchasers in cardboard boxes stamped *kenko kigu* (health apparatus), and users are assured of lifelong after-service. While the vow "until death us do part" may be stretching things a bit, however, the company also anticipates a time when Jewel might outlive her usefulness—or her owner.

"If a *yome* (bride) is no longer needed, we'll discretely take her off a customer's hands at no charge," Tsuchiya adds. "Twice a year we also arrange for a *kuyo* Buddhist memorial service for discarded dolls at the special bodhisattva for dolls at the Shimizu Kannon-do in Ueno Park." Founded in 1631, it's where the "souls" of dolls are consecrated. (Kannon is the Goddess of Mercy.)

This devoted treatment, says Tsuchiya, is out of deference to his customers' frequent close emotional attachment to their Dutch wives. Which may not necessarily be a bad thing. When Tsuchiya reads of a teacher or policeman nabbed for molesting a woman, or perverts who hold girls in extended confinement, he sighs to himself, "If only they had owned one of our girls, they wouldn't have committed such a crime!" (MS)

THEY SAID IT IN THE *Weeklies*

"We drew on the greatest minds of the adult toy business to come up with Vicon. We sent one of our workers out to brothels on numerous occasions to do research on women and find out the average location of the clitoris. We're confident that it will be of an ideal size and correct placement for every single person."

—A spokesman for the developer of Vicon, short for "vibrator condom," tells *Shukan Gendai* about the revolutionary invention (October 16, 2004)

OVERSEXED SALARYMEN GO BROKE

Shukan Jitsuwa (May 27, 2004)

For one 33-year-old real-estate agent, the road to financial ruin began last autumn.

"My boss had invited me to a low-priced soapland (massage parlor) in Shinjuku. When we arrived, there was this fantastically beautiful woman. She had the triple whammy of face, long legs and sexuality," sighs the man, whose name is not disclosed. "Plus she was nice and quickly made me forget all the stress from my job."

In no time, the real-estate agent became the woman's regular patron. However, his infatuation quickly turned into an expensive addiction, which first emptied his wallet and then his savings account. "I borrowed a total of ¥4 million from five loan-shark agencies. But now that I can't pay it back, I've hired a lawyer for personal-bankruptcy proceedings," he says.

The real-estate agent is just one of a growing number of salarymen whose obsession with massage parlors, cheap hostess bars and other sex establishments has driven them into financial insolvency, according to *Shukan Jitsuwa.*

What's remarkable about the trend is that paid sex is actually a lot cheaper now than in recent years. Since Japan's economic bubble burst well over a decade ago, sex establishments have been forced to cut prices in line with the slimmer wallets of their customers. Yet the problem for the salarymen—never mind their wives—is that the sex industry did an excessively good job in adapting to the leaner economic times.

A writer specializing in the sex industry explains: "Amid the fierce competition, the establishments realized that if being cheaper meant getting worse, then they would lose customers. So they actually improved their quality. Young women can now be selected by the customer for reasonable prices in *kyabare* (cabaret) bars (where quick and low-priced sexual services are offered along with the drinks) and the guys have jumped all over such inducements."

IT has helped make such inducements all the more irresistible. Many establishments run websites that profile their female workers, and in the process have turned the women into starlets known by hundreds, if not thousands, of guys across the country, the magazine says. The best-known ones make special appearances in cabarets throughout Japan, where they are mobbed by local fans. Conversely, some customers have been known to take the bullet train to distant cities for the chance of a face-to-face meeting with the objects of their fantasies. Now couple all that with the proliferation of camera-equipped cell phones, and a phenomenon is born.

"All of the customers have these phones," says the manager of a cabaret in the Tokyo district of Shibuya. "In the beginning we got requests asking if they could use them to take photos of the women naked. So now we allow picture-taking, depending on how often the customer has come here. We think it's helped improve our sales."

As a result of these developments, the average working stiff is offered lower prices with greater choice. The former attracts them. The latter keeps them hooked. And for many such customers, it takes nothing short of personal bankruptcy to force them to let go. (GB)

RESORT'S APPEAL IS SEX, SEX, SEX

Shukan Jitsuwa (September 16, 2004)

Located halfway down the Ise Peninsula in Mie Prefecture—some two hours by train and car from Nagoya—the island of Watakano is unlikely to be tabbed for a Club Med resort.

Its location, which is far off the beaten track, does have certain attractions: For well over a century, this scenic little island, 7 km (4.3 miles) in circumference, has been a hotbed of prostitution.

A company employee in his 40s who pays monthly visits to the isolated island tells *Shukan Jitsuwa* that the females who sell their charms to tourists are now mostly Japanese. "Until not too long ago, the place was much more cosmopolitan," he recalls. "There were Chinese, Filipinas, Thais—even Colombians and Russians."

That changed about four years ago, when most of the foreigners were rounded up by immigration authorities. "Now, it's more than 80 percent Japanese," the man says. "And due to an ongoing shortage of sex workers, there's been an influx of girls from Osaka and Kobe who are more like part-timers than pros."

An estimated 50 women work out of the island's 10 *okiya* (houses of assignation), where the pleasure of their company runs between ¥20,000 to ¥40,000. "Since they're paid on a percentage basis, when no customers are around, there's nothing for them to do but leave the island," the man explains. "But popular girls get pretty regular overnight business. In fact, it's not rare to see them marrying their customers."

Day-time visitors to the island would be largely clueless to the locale's traditional industry, as the women tend to remain out of sight during daylight hours. Some of the women take the short ferry ride to the mainland to shop or play pachinko.

"The girls mostly sleep during the day and go to work after the sun goes down," a local explains. Matchmaking is performed by several elderly procuresses, who cruise the town's short main street and direct arriving male customers to the nearby shops.

"My objective is to save up a bundle," says a 29-year-old woman who entertained *Shukan Jitsuwa*'s reporter in a six-mat tatami room near the pier. "My girlfriend saved ¥5 million in one year. She convinced me to come here and work. It's not so much the money's that good—more like there's nowhere here to spend it; no aesthetic treatment salons and no host clubs. So I just work nights and sleep days, one day after the next.

"And I prepare my own meals. Seafood around here is cheap and tasty; but I don't get any real exercise, unless you call doing *that* exercise. So I've put on quite a bit of weight since coming here."

Watakano has made efforts to diversify its attractions and they may finally be paying off. A year ago the island opened a man-made swimming beach. "Its got showers and new facilities, just like a modern resort," a mainland taxi driver tells the magazine. "In the old days, only men went there to get women. Now you see lots of young families. It's metamorphosing into a wholesome tourist destination."

And one where, one could rightly conclude, the recreational facilities are as different as night and day. (MS)

WOMEN SELL SELVES ABROAD, KEEP FACE

Spa! (December 14, 2004)

Yoko Kimizuka, a 27-year-old temp staffer in Osaka, was in a bind—financially speaking. To fund her lavish lifestyle, she had borrowed a total of ¥1.5 million from seven consumer-loan companies, which were hounding her to repay the money.

The problem was, she couldn't—at least not on her meager salary. As her debts piled up, her only option was to declare personal bankruptcy, it seemed. But that was before she spotted a magazine ad placed by a financial broker that promised to put an end to young women's debts. "When I phoned and went for an interview, he said he could consolidate my debts," Kimizuka tells *Spa!*

The big hitch in all this—she had to work in South Korea's local sex industry. "But they said I would never be found out while working over there. I also thought it would be a great chance to learn *Hangul* (Korean writing)," Kimizuka says cheerily.

So off she went. "My work was in an extremely exclusive club, and all the customers were wonderful," she says. Within four months, she not only earned enough to repay her debts but also managed to save ¥400,000. "I am grateful to the financial broker. I'd love to go again if the opportunity comes up," she says.

According to the article, Kimizuka is one of a rapidly growing number of Japanese women snapping up such opportunities. The magazine discovers that Japan, infamous for being one of the world's biggest importers of sex workers, has recently become something of an exporter as well. Today, young Japanese women are working as prostitutes not only in South Korea, but also in the United

States, Australia and Thailand, to name just a few countries.

Kimizuka's case is typical for many, if not most, of these women. They go overseas with the aim of working for several months to pay off large debts. Why not do the same in Japan? Because, as Kimizuka's broker points out, if they are working abroad the chance of friends or relatives back in Japan finding out about their adopted profession is close to zero. And when they leave Japan, they can go under the guise of students or long-term tourists.

Ken Kitashiba, a former police investigator turned writer, points to a well-established underground network that facilitates the flow of Japanese women to South Korea and other countries.

"The organized crime groups in the Kansai region have long had resident Koreans in their ranks, and the Kansai mob and the South Korean mafia have been on friendly terms for decades," he explains.

Most of the demand for the services of Japanese women in foreign countries are from Japanese expats and tourists, Kitashiba says. "The Japanese men in these countries are often afraid that the local women have diseases. That's why the Japanese women are treasured so much."

Yet a significant number of the women are also doing plenty of business with the local men, *Spa!* says. "Over there, men go crazy for the chance to have sex with an 'oriental,'" says Kuniko Saito, who claims to have earned more than ¥10 million during the year she spent in New Jersey. "For American men, a fair complexion with straight hair and black eyes is a fantasy," she says, adding that she promptly restored her once permed and dyed hair to its natural state soon after starting her overseas gig.

What amazes *Spa!* is that none of the women interviewed seem to feel any guilt or shame over their activities. Rather, they all describe their overseas experiences as exciting—and even fulfilling—adventures. (GB)

III

A Matter of Taste

GLUTTONY THRIVES ON AIR WAVES

Shukan Jitsuwa (December 6, 2001)

The trendsetter's wreath goes to the TV Tokyo network. Theirs was the idea to stack heaps of food in front of people, have them tear into it, and call it entertainment. Not very clever, even somewhat gross, perhaps, but the prime-time audience disagreed, tuning in with such consuming eagerness that "TV Champion" quickly became the broadcast industry's role model. Unabashed imitation followed. NTV weighed in with "Food Fight," TBS with "Food Battle Club," and so on. "It's enough to give you heartburn!" fumes *Shukan Jitsuwa*.

Gluttony became art, and gluttons became *"talento"* (celebrities), one of whom, "tubby tarento" Shinji Uchiyama, distinguished himself by eating his way through all 100 items on a five-star Chinese restaurant's menu.

Nothing beats a TV food fight, as the NTV network knows from bitter experience. Once, says *Shukan Jitsuwa*, it even tried pitting the popular program "Magical Intelligence Power" against TV Tokyo's "TV Champion." No dice. "Magical Intelligence" bit the dust.

Unseemly spectacles on screen spawn unseemlier ones off, as the rival networks headhunt each others' star gluttons. Imagine how TV Tokyo felt when TBS lured "glutton idol" Takashi Kobayashi with prize money of ¥5 million—against TV Tokyo's ¥500,000!

To all this, the magazine raises objections both medical and social. Medically speaking, it is the rare digestive tract that can withstand unscathed consumption totally out of sync with one's natural appetite.

The social objections are twofold. First, the stardom that on-camera gorging confers is bright but tarnished. One female eating champ enjoys her celebrity status but won no points with her boyfriend's family, who cringed at the thought of their son marrying a woman of such "vulgar" occupation. In a similar vein, a male TV glutton's fame reflected darkly on his young son, who was bullied mercilessly at school.

A more trenchant case for the tastelessness of gluttony as entertainment was made in a sharply worded letter *Shukan Jitsuwa* received from a reader: "Let them contribute the million-yen prize money to Afghanistan instead!"

Good point. How to justify force-feeding stars for laughs and prizes while masses of people, some of them lately visible on the same screens in the same living rooms, suffer and starve?

The magazine takes up the argument with the networks and, predictably, wins no converts. One TV executive castigates the "confused logic" of mixing apples and oranges. "News is news, entertainment is entertainment," he says. Another put it this way: "We must produce programs that appeal to sponsors. That means appealing to young women. Sponsors know that if they get high school girls and OLs buying, the men will follow. Programs about travel, cooking and eating are low-budget yet draw large audiences."

In short, Afghanistan or no, performance food-stuffing is here to stay. (MH)

YOUNG WIVES ASSAULT BUDS

Shukan Taishu (June 24, 2002)

Feeling peckish? Then how about some instant ramen smothered in ketchup? Or perhaps raw *katsuo* (bonito) drowned in cooking oil? For dessert, nothing beats *soba* noodles in chocolate sauce.

Unfortunately, the above menu items are no joke. *Shukan Taishu* has discovered that those are but a few of the stomach-churning concoctions that young housewives are serving their menfolk these days.

Working men used to look forward to coming home to such healthy and tasty dishes as *niku jaga* (a stew of potatoes and thinly sliced beef in soy sauce and sake) or *hijiki nimono* (fried and simmered seaweed). These days, however, the family dinner table is more likely to contain an assortment of unsavory offerings chock-full of oil, salt, artificial preservatives and god knows what else. The problem, as the magazine sees it, is that young housewives are losing their common sense when it comes to good cooking, particularly when it comes to choosing the right ingredients.

"My wife started putting mayonnaise with everything about two or three years ago—rice, bread, grilled meat and fish, pasta, ramen, *udon*," grumbles a 28-year-old company employee. "Recently she's been putting hot mayonnaise on sashimi. Can you believe that?"

Another guy, a 23-year-old salaryman, recalls the shock he felt after trying out a new type of *gyoza* (Chinese meat dumpling), that his wife whipped up one day. "After I ate one, the taste of mint suddenly spread throughout my mouth, and it made me throw up. When I asked what was going on, she explained that she had put five or six breath-freshening mint tablets in each dumpling to get rid of garlic breath." It was enough to make him seriously consider divorce.

A 35-year-old who works in finance complains of his wife's obsession with anything sweet. "She eats rice after mixing it with carbonated drinks like cola or cider. She says it makes her mouth feel refreshed," he says. A typical dessert at the couple's home is cheesecake containing a few drops of soy sauce ("to give it a kick"), served with a glass of Japanese tea mixed with an equal amount of milk.

"In many cases, these kinds of people are suffering from an illness that has damaged their sense of taste," says the unnamed editor of a health magazine. "There are young people who skip breakfast, eat a convenience store *bento* for lunch and in the evening have cup noodles. As a result they develop zinc deficiencies, and eventually they no longer taste anything."

Shukan Taishu says the breakdown of the traditional family structure is largely to blame for this state of affairs. Back when it was common for three generations to live under the same roof, meals tended to be elaborate and communal affairs.

Yumi Yamashita, an author who has written about people's eating habits, believes that fixing the ongoing "chaos over cuisine" will require getting back to some basics. "It's important to gather the ingredients and prepare the meals by oneself," she says. "Families need to sit down together when they eat, and their meals should reflect the seasons." (GB)

RAW BOTTOMS ON CHINESE MENU

Shukan Gendai (March 1, 2003)

During the heady years of the Bubble Economy, Loulan, an exclusive *shabu-shabu* restaurant in Tokyo's Shinjuku district, became the venue of choice for top businessmen. With lavish expense accounts, they wined and dined Finance Ministry bureaucrats and other influential figures.

Loulan's *pièce de résistance* was not just its mouth-watering slivers of tender, thinly sliced beef from pampered *wagyu* steers, but its fetching young waitresses, who served customers clad in a blouse, apron and skimpy miniskirt with nothing underneath. Loulan managed to entertain male guests in a variety of imaginative ways. When refilling a customer's wine glass, for example, a waitress would have to reach high over her head and pull down a bottle suspended by rope from the ceiling, so as to provide the leering diners with an uplifting view.

Alas, Loulan is no more. Its owner, Nobuyuki Konno, was arrested in 1998 and several of its waitresses were charged with committing obscene acts. Still, old habits die hard. With so much Japanese investment flowing into China nowadays, Shanghai entrepreneurs have emulated Loulan with their own *no-pan* ("no pants") shabu-shabu restaurant in what is clearly a shameless attempt to transplant Japan's corporate culture overseas.

The restaurant, reports *Shukan Gendai*'s correspondent, is located in the high-tech Pudong district, across the Huangpu River from the old part of Shanghai. Based on a three-hour system, guests can dine on sukiyaki or shabu-shabu for 300 yuan (¥4,500) per person, with drinks additional. A customer also pays 300 yuan for each waitress in attendance.

The meal is taken in a spacious private room, seated around a table with a *hori-kotatsu* (sunken hearth). The two male customers are served by three leggy young attendants.

Sneaking a sidelong glance while being served, the magazine's reporter notes with disappointment that it would appear the shop falls short of its claim to adorn its staff in the same uniform as did Loulan. But as the main course gives way to dessert, things begin to loosen up, including the elastic waistbands holding up the girls' underthings. As it turns out, the call of duty goes above—and beyond—anything ever offered in Japan.

"We've got rooms upstairs," a waitress named Meimei murmurs to the visiting reporter. "I'll go with you for ¥10,000."

According to a Japanese journalist based in Shanghai, local girls who have been to Japan for language study can readily find employment in such establishments. "Before, girls usually worked at these jobs out of genuine economic need," he says. "But these days, most of them just want money to buy designer-brand goods or to have a good time. Even students from Shanghai Jiaotong University, President Jiang Zemin's alma mater, work at these places during their summer vacation."

The pleasures of the ladies' company, however, come with certain caveats: Chinese authorities sometimes conduct sweeps, and foreigners caught with their own pants down risk detention or expulsion from the country.

"I suppose the place is run by some local big shot who's persuaded the cops to look the other way," suggests Mo Bangfu, a Japan-based Chinese journalist. "It might look Japanese, but if you let down your guard, you could get badly burned." (MS)

WEALTHY EATERS LARGEST WASTERS

Shukan Economist (November 18, 2003)

"The destiny of a nation depends on the manner in which it feeds itself," wrote Jean-Anthelme Brillat-Savarin (1755–1826) in his famous treatise "The Physiology of Taste: Or Meditations on Transcendental Gastronomy."

One is moved to wonder what Brillat-Savarin might have remarked about the destiny of today's Japan. Takaaki Fukayama, for one, is dismayed. Writing in the business magazine *Shukan Economist*, Fukayama, a member of the Japanese Society for Sensory Evaluation, points out that although Japan imports approximately 60 percent of its foodstuffs, it leaves behind a shocking amount unconsumed.

Statistical data show that while supplied calories have remained largely unchanged from the mid-1970s, intake has gradually declined. Out of each 2642.1 kilocalories served to individuals in 2000, only 1,948 were consumed, leaving a gap of nearly 700 kilocalories. This means, in effect, that a quarter of what's served on the nation's plate winds up in the trash.

It's ironic that while Japan despairs over the "missing decade" that occurred following the collapse of the economic bubble in the early 1990s, another bubble, one of waste, continues to swell. The United States—where obesity is reaching epidemic proportions— was at one time even worse; but since 1995 its waste has declined, leaving Japan with the dubious distinction of being the world's No. 1 squanderer of food on a per capita basis.

Granted, some 10 percent of this waste is recycled, or processed into fertilizer or animal feed. But this comes to just 10 percent of the total volume discarded, and the remaining 90 percent, or 17.27 million tons, gets burned or is bulldozed into land fills.

All this waste, moreover, wreaks havoc on the environment, including the generation of deadly dioxins through the combustion of plastics. And people may very well be eating themselves into an earlier grave. The consumption of processed foods is causing the clogging of even young people's arteries and triggering osteoporosis in women of an increasingly younger age.

The Agriculture, Forestry and Fisheries Ministry, which compiles statistics on so-called "food loss," has made its findings public since March 2001. This data shows that about 23.9 percent of the food served at wedding banquets winds up in the trash. At ordinary banquets, waste only comes to 15.7 percent.

In homes, 7.7 percent is discarded, including food tossed out for reasons ranging from expiration of the consumption date to simply preparing more than the family can consume. Restaurants and dining halls, by contrast, are the least wasteful at 3.6 percent.

The *o-bento* (box lunches) sold by convenience stores may be the worst offenders of all. Including rice, the value of prepared food discarded at your average convenience store due to expiration of freshness is estimated at ¥10,000 to ¥15,000 per day. Multiplied by 40,823 *konbini* stores in Japan, that brings the waste, in retail terms, to a staggering ¥220 billion per year. And even if only calculated in terms of the cost of materials, it still comes to approximately ¥66 billion just for box lunches alone.

This level of profligacy is highlighted by *Shukan Economist*'s shocking revelation that the volume of food discarded by convenience stores and supermarkets due to passing of the expiry date—an estimated six million tons per year—is equivalent to roughly *80 percent* of the total volume of food assistance currently being supplied to needy countries, or enough to feed 50 million people for a year. Transposing calories into monetary values, Japan's food losses are roughly equal to the total annual output of its agricultural and fishery industries.

To add insult to injury, while millions in the world go hungry, Japan's print media and television continue to eagerly promote latest trends in gourmet dining or host contests that award prizes for gluttony—a situation, Fukayama gravely pronounces, analogous to "a splendid pavilion built on a foundation of sand." (MS)

THEY SAID IT IN THE *Weeklies*

"Rats have occupied Tokyo. The densely packed buildings are perfect homes for them. Western cities worked hard to exterminate them, but it's almost like we're going out of our way to make life comfortable for them. Tokyo is the only city in the industrialized world where the vermin are on the increase."

—Rat researcher Tatsuo Yabe, to *Shukan Taishu* (September 6, 2004)

FAST FOOD SHRINKS EXECS' LIFESPAN

Shukan Taishu (July 2, 2004)

Mr. A, an office worker in his late 30s, waits in a line outside a busy *gyudon* restaurant near Shinbashi Station in Tokyo. His choice of lunch, a few thin slices of fatty beef on a mountain of rice at one of the country's largest fast-food chains, is a matter of economics. "My allowance has been cut because our mortgage is really harsh. Still, I can have lunch nowadays for about the same price as a pack of cigarettes and that's a big help," he says.

For Mr. A and thousands of other working stiffs like him, fast food is becoming standard lunchtime fare. Helping to drive the trend is a fierce price war among several of Japan's fast-food chains, a boon to workers who have endured a decade of hard economic times.

As for their health, however, it's been anything but a blessing, *Shukan Taishu* warns. A survey released this month by the Ministry of Health, Labor and Welfare finds that the health of Japanese men in their 30s and 40s (who are in the middle of their careers) has worsened during the past decade. Women and men in other age groups, on the other hand, are healthier than before.

The problem with eating fast food is that gyudon, hamburgers and other such items are prepared with large amounts of salt, which acts as a preservative. Salt triggers high blood pressure, which is especially dangerous because it is a silent killer. Sufferers are usually unaware they have the ailment until it's too late—like when they are struck down by debilitating strokes.

The effects of excessive salt can be counteracted by ordering a salad or fresh side dishes. However, cash-strapped salarymen on their lunch breaks tend to stick to a single greasy main item.

Add to this the socioeconomic factor. The money that salarymen use to buy their lunches usually comes out of a set monthly allowance doled out by their wives (who most often control the family finances). However, many working guys have seen their allowances slashed in response to belt-tightening at home, a move that in turn stems from the prolonged recession.

Consider the plight of Mr. B, 40, who works for an auto sales company. "In April, I was informed by my wife that my allowance would drop by ¥5,000 to pay the fees for my kids' cram school," he says, adding that he is now forced to live off ¥20,000 a month. "That's ¥800 a day, which comprises lunch money. A complete lunch is really out of the question."

Mr. B is not alone. A survey by Mizuho Securities Co. finds the average allowance of breadwinners is just under ¥20,000 a month, roughly the same as it was 20 years ago.

Yet the situation is far from hopeless for white-collar workers on dietary budgets. The magazine's advice is simple–eat fruit and vegetables along with your meals. And get as much exercise as possible, even if that means walking to nearby destinations rather than taking a subway. Then you can use the money saved on the tickets to buy a decent lunch for once. (GB)

SOMETHING FISHY WITH SUSHI

Shukan Post (October 29, 2004)

It's late afternoon, and in Tokyo's ultratrendy district of Harajuku, a long line has formed in front of a *kaiten,* or conveyor-belt, sushi bar.

An electronic signboard informs those in the queue of a "30-minute wait," even though this time of day—too late for lunch, too early for dinner—is usually a dead zone, business-wise.

But ask the customers, and the reason why they are so keen on getting inside, no matter what the hour, becomes clear: sushi, long considered an expensive delicacy, selling for nearly fast-food prices.

"It's great for me—a bill for my family of four comes to less than ¥3,000," says one breadwinner, who is happy to wait up to half an hour at the Harajuku restaurant. Another satisfied customer says, "We can try out all sorts of fish that we don't normally eat, and we can get it really cheap."

It's those kind of perceptions that have made kaiten sushi one of the most popular dining-out experiences throughout the country. The number of shops nationwide has ballooned to around 5,000, and they do about ¥500 billion of business annually.

Yet *Shukan Post* detects something definitely fishy in all this. How can the restaurants offer sushi dishes for such low prices, when their ingredients sell for a fortune at the markets?

An extensive investigation into the kaiten sushi boom reveals some shocking answers, which are explained in two long articles in successive editions. In short, the magazine finds, the business is riddled with deception, in particular the flagrant mislabeling of fish and shellfish on restaurant menus.

Take tuna, for instance. The two basic types are *maguro,* a sushi staple, and the more expensive *toro,* which comes from the soft and fatty underbelly. The former is red, the latter pink.

Toro is popular when prepared as *negitoro,* in which the fish is minced and mixed with sliced leeks. Customers at sushi restaurants are often amazed at the low price of negitoro, given that its main ingredient is such a delicacy.

Or is it?

Not according to one anonymous chef at an exclusive sushi restaurant in Tokyo's Roppongi district.

"That's just made by mixing the red maguro with oil," he says.

In fact, there's a special type of oil sold to sushi restaurants: It is a pale yellow, resembling the color of margarine, and turns red maguro into the light pink of toro.

According to another expert sushi chef the differences in flavor and texture between this concoction and the real thing are miles apart.

"Real negitoro uses *dai-toro* (the best toro of all), so it has a neutral sweet smell with a maguro flavor. It melts when you eat it," he says.

"However, this fake type of negitoro has an oily smell and no trace of maguro flavor. Fish oil melts at body temperature, but this is like eating oil."

It's a similar story with many of the other varieties of fish served up at kaiten sushi bars.

Nile perch, which inhabits rivers in Africa, is passed off as *suzuki,* a type of sea perch found off Japan's shores. The African type sells for around ¥20 a pair at wholesale markets in Japan. The genuine suzuki sells at ¥45 a piece for farmed fish and ¥90 for the natural variety.

Awabi, or abalone, one of the most popular types of shellfish among sushi aficionados, is often just *roko-gai*, a similar-looking, but not similar-tasting, shellfish commonly found in South America. Their wholesale prices are ¥770 per pair compared to ¥60, respectively.

Shukan Post lists five types of fish and three types of shellfish that are commonly substituted by cheaper products.

The magazine pins much of the problem of menu deception on fierce competition among sushi bars, which has induced operators to slash prices to unfeasibly low levels.

"If you want to sell an item for ¥100, it's going to be extremely difficult to use the real item," says an executive of a seafood distributor, whose name is not disclosed. "This has even led to the development of a market of substitute fish just for kaiten sushi."

Shukan Post's disclosures are sure to disappoint many a kaiten-sushi fan. But then, they should have realized long ago that if something is too good to be true—"like toro at maguro prices"—it probably isn't. (GB)

THEY SAID IT IN THE *Weeklies*

"We knew we needed to come up with a different line of business. We ran a normal hot dog joint for about a year, before deciding to start using ice cream instead of franks."

—"Ice dog" creator Eiko Arai to *Shukan Taishu* (December 27, 2004)

FAST-FOOD COMPETITION PROVES DEADLY

Weekly Playboy (November 18, 2004)

"It was just too dangerous. From our point of view, it was not the kind of competition that should ever have been held."

Japan has its share of extreme sports fraught with danger, but the deadly competition Kenji Aoki, a professional eater, was talking about was a bread-eating contest in the otherwise sleepy Hyogo Prefecture town of Fukusaki that claimed the life of a 38-year-old housewife who literally bit off more than she could chew.

Fukusaki Chamber of Commerce held the fatal contest on November 6 to promote *mochimugi*, a glutinous type of wheat and a local specialty. Competitors had to battle it out to be the fastest to eat one slice of bread, two pieces of cake, a candy, a bowl of noodles and a rice ball, all of which were made with the chewy mochimugi.

"Dry, crumby food like bread or cakes absorbs the saliva and causes the throat to block. They're difficult foods to eat quickly even for experienced competitors. A junior high school pupil choked to death a couple of years ago during a bread roll eating contest," Aoki, who makes a living out of being able to ravenously gobble food in the shortest possible time, tells *Weekly Playboy*. "World Champion Hot Dog Eater Takeru Kobayashi always takes a sip of water so the bread he eats doesn't get caught in his throat. The Fukusaki contest involved eating a small amount of food in the quickest possible time. It basically encourages people to shove as much in their mouth as possible to get it down as soon as they can. This invites blockages as people try to gobble up more than they should."

Organizers from the Fukusaki Chamber of Commerce who did not have a doctor on standby and offered a measly ¥2,000 first prize in the competition say economics played a huge role in what happened on that fateful day.

"If we were only going to give out samples, we would have had to prepare enormous quantities of food, costing an impermissible amount of time and money. We felt that if we held an eating contest, we'd be able to get by just preparing enough food for the 50 people who actually took part," a chamber spokesman tells the magazine. "We didn't know at the time that a schoolboy had died in a bread eating contest some time back. A chamber volunteer who ate all the items on the menu as a test for the contest took four minutes to get through them with no worries, so we assumed it would be safe. We'll look after the woman's family in an appropriate manner, but there was nothing wrong with the way we ran the contest and the organizers bear absolutely no responsibility for what happened." (RC)

THEY SAID IT IN THE *Weeklies*

"We just want Yu to be alive. He's 14 months old but looks much younger. I don't know why anyone would want to steal him. We had him since he was an egg, so it's not just about the money."

—A worker at the Furaku Yu home for the mentally disabled, after one of their pet ostriches—used as therapy—was stolen, to *Shukan Shincho* (July 1, 2004)

ANGRY COMMUTERS TURN DEADLY

Sunday Mainichi (June 3, 2001)

One evening aboard Tokyo's Tozai subway line, businessman Yoshio Morita heard a scream. He turned to see three youths slapping the face of a girl of about the same age.

"Hey, stop that," the 45-year-old Morita admonished them. "You shouldn't hit girls."

"Beat it, pops," one responded gruffly. The two exchanged hostile glares.

"My mistake was thinking they were just kids," Morita relates to a journalist from *Sunday Mainichi*. "By the time I got off the train and walked out of the station, they'd used their cell phones to summon more than 10 of their pals and ganged up on me . . ."

Under the ensuing assault, Morita suffered several broken ribs and was robbed of ¥30,000. "I was saved because somebody called the police," he says. "I still get chills down my spine recalling it."

The railways insist it's not their fight. But the once-sporadic acts of violence on Japan's public transport system are becoming widespread. From 1,564 incidents of aggravated assault reported in 1998, the National Police Agency notes the number rose to 1,618 in 1999 and 2,377 last year. As these cover only reported crimes, the actual figures are thought to be several times higher.

"Social stress is the main factor," observes psychiatrist-author Seiji Mori. "The prolonged recession, job layoffs, family tensions and so on are causing anger to build up. People are unaware of their inner urge to let fly all at once."

Japan's postwar generation has less experience in exercising forbearance, adds Mori. "It's easy for them to react to even a slight stimulation—they have a low flash point. And a packed train is the place where all these adverse factors come together."

"Many incidents happen when people get drunk," says Masao Hikima, team leader of the Tokyo branch of the Guardian Angels, a volunteer group transplanted from the U.S. to curb street crime.

Aware of the growing problem, railway companies have begun adopting new measures. The operator of Tokyo's Oedo subway, which opened last December, dispatches at least seven plainclothes security guards to patrol its trains. Odakyu Railways, meanwhile, requests over its trains' PA systems that passengers report any trouble to a conductor or station worker.

If a tight situation does occur, what's the best response?

"There isn't much an average person can do, aside from raising his voice," says Guardian Angels' Hikima. "Putting up a weak defense is more likely to have the opposite effect on an assailant. Shouting 'Stop!' or 'Help me!' attracts notice."

But isn't it a fact, counters the *Sunday Mainichi*, that most people won't get involved? "That's definitely a problem," Hikima agrees. "One of our group's main goals is to appeal to people to stop looking the other way."

Preventative measures came too late for one victim. Just past midnight on the evening of April 28, bank worker Akira Maki, 43, exchanged angry words with four youths aboard the Denentoshi Line. When he stomped off the train at Sangenjaya Station, the four followed him onto the platform and beat him senseless. Maki expired from a brain injury six days later.

A former classmate recalled that Maki had an outspoken character and strongly developed sense of right and wrong. "At a bar, if some customer raised a ruckus, Akira would tell him to quiet down. And if his boss made a mistake, he never hesitated to let him know."

The dispute that led to Maki's death appears to have arisen after someone trod upon someone else's foot. "It was just a little spat. I can't understand why it had to come to that," murmurs the victim's older brother. "If they had just broken an arm or something, he would have recovered. But you can't replace a lost life." (MS)

NINJA MOLESTERS STRIKE YEAR-ROUND

Shukan Taishu (December 3, 2001)

For the thousands of serial molesters nationwide, the approaching winter may seem a depressing prospect. With the days getting colder, young women are choosing the warmth of home, safe from molesters' groping hands. When they do venture outside, dressing in several layers of nearly impenetrable clothing is *de rigueur.*

Yet none of this is a matter of concern for what *Shukan Taishu* calls the "winter *chikan"*—chikan meaning men who enjoy groping women in public places. For these are a dedicated and resourceful lot, according to Samu Yamamoto, a self-confessed serial molester and author of several books on the way of the chikan.

"You would think that it's a tough season, what with women guarding themselves with thick coats and sweaters," he says. "Yet for some chikan pros, it's also a season to get excited about."

Winter chikan employ all the stealth and resourcefulness of ninja. For instance, they will make sure to warm their hands, as contact from cold hands can cause unwanted surprise from their victims. And to avoid electrical shocks, which often occur when one touches nylon stockings in the dry air of winter, they apply an antistatic spray to their hands. *Shukan Taishu* talks to a number of "currently active" wintertime molesters for additional insights.

Take Mineo Orita, who is 39 and has been molesting women for the past 13 years. His favorite winter hunting ground are *hatsumode*, New Year temple and shrine events that attract huge crowds. Orita usually makes his move while his unfortunate victims are right in front of the main temple or shrine hall, concentrating on either throwing coins into the donation box or praying.

"There is a huge mass of people behind them, and I move in sync with the pushing of the crowd. The secret is to make it look like your movements are involuntary," he says.

Yoshio Asakura, 32, preys on the primly uniformed young women who operate elevators at department stores. The women have no choice but to leave themselves vulnerable to the likes of chikan, as they face away from the crowd in the elevator to operate its controls. Our groper, of course, always tries to secure the nearest position behind the women and uses shopping bags to obscure the movement of his hands.

Other molesters operate under the cover of darkness. Toshihiko Sasaki, 49, has been prowling movie theaters for the past couple of decades. "The theaters are warm, so people take off their coats. I come up behind women who stand while watching the movies and feel their bums," he says. In the event that he is found out, the darkness provides an effective cover for escape.

It should be noted that this pulpy men's mag is largely unsympathetic to the plight of the female victims. Although its final statement is a don't-try-this-at-home warning, it's a matter of some concern whether readers take that to heart or instead use the article's information for their own nefarious purposes. Molesting women is, after all, illegal in Japan. (GB)

Friday (December 28, 2001)

The judge and jurors take their seats. The date: December 5. The Vladivostok branch of Russia's Maritime Territory Court is now in session. In the dock—the cage, rather—are three men. The charge? Conspiring to do to Japan something like what al-Qaeda did to the United States.

The three defendants are Dmitri Shigachev, 24, Sergei Topeko, 28, and Dmitri Voronov, 32. They are accused—and admit the substance of the accusation, writes journalist Yoichiro Aonuma in *Friday*—of having plotted to bomb various locations in Tokyo in a bid to spring Aum Shinrikyo guru Shoko Asahara from prison.

Banned in 1995 after the cult's lethal sarin gas attack on Tokyo subway commuters, Aum's Russian branch nonetheless maintains a shadowy existence, with some 300 believers in Moscow performing devotions under the supervision of four Japanese Aum priests. (In Japan, Aum now calls itself Aleph.)

Shigachev, the youngest of the three defendants, is the trio's leader. In 1999 he used the Internet to recruit collaborators for a daring plan he had conceived. The logic was simple. "Asahara," co-defendant Topeko told the court, "should be free. Since there were no legal means to free him, we had no choice but to use terrorism and violence to demand his release."

Flush with funds from an Aum-affiliated Japanese entrepreneur Shigachev met in Phuket, Thailand, the little group set to work. Topeko procured the weaponry. Voronov, a Vladivostok used-tire salesman, made local preparations, securing a garage to hide the arms in, renting an apartment-hideout for Asahara, and so on. In December 1999, Shigachev and Topeko rode the Trans-Siberian Railway from Moscow to Vladivostok with three sandbags filled with hand grenades, handmade bombs, Tokarev and Kalashnikov firearms and ammunition. The following March, Shigachev traveled to Tokyo to scout the terrain.

Bombs were to be placed at Ueno Station, Shibuya Parco, a Shinjuku high-rise, a Shinagawa hotel, and in a gas storage facility of the Tokyo Detention Center, where Asahara was being held. Then the Japanese government would be warned: Free Asahara, or expose the metropolis to devastating death and destruction. Meanwhile, eerily foreshadowing the flying lessons taken by the September 11 hijackers, the three men apparently took boating lessons as part of their preparations to spirit Asahara across the Sea of Japan to Russia.

What motivated them? "My son," Aonuma hears from Voronov's Chechen mother, "was working with an oil exploration team in Chechnya when he fell from a tower. The doctors could do nothing for him. He visited Asahara, and in three days his injuries healed. That's when he became a believer. We escaped the Chechen war. In Russia we were recognized as refugees, but were given no support. We drifted to Vladivostok. There was nothing here either. I can understand why my son became involved in something like this . . ."

What would have happened had the three not been arrested on July 1 by Russian police acting on "secret information"? We're lucky not to know. (MH)

BRUTAL TEEN KILLER RELEASED

Dias (January 31, 2002)

"Seito Sakakibara, Shool [sic] Killer"—that's the twisted name a 14-year-old gave himself back in May 1997, as he played cat-and-mouse with police investigating the murder of two small Kobe children. One of the children had been decapitated, his head placed in front of a junior high school to greet the area's earliest risers. It took a month to solve the case. The sheer ghastliness of the crime threw detectives off the track. Surely only a very disturbed man could have committed it? No one thought, at first, of a very disturbed boy.

He's 19 now, going on 20, and the Juvenile Law under which his rehabilitation has been proceeding will soon no longer apply to him. This spring, says *Dias*, Seito Sakakibara rejoins society. Is he ready? Are we?

Secrecy veils him, as it must if he is to have any kind of a future. Even the location of the facility currently holding him is unknown. Once released, where will he live? Under what name? In whose custody? In what occupation? We don't know.

And the most important question of all: Is he cured? *Dias* speaks at length with Yoshikuni Noguchi, a lawyer who has interviewed Sakakibara often. Noguchi is guardedly optimistic. He was struck during their earliest meetings at a Kobe detention center by the utterly blank expression on Sakakibara's face. The boy showed no emotion at all.

"He was like no one I'd ever met," Noguchi recalls. "Apparently he had no values of his own, and no perception of anyone else's.

He could kill himself, or kill others, with perfect equanimity."

A year later Noguchi interviewed Sakakibara again, this time at the Youth Correction Center in Fuchu, Tokyo. Sakakibara was expressionless as usual—until the end of the session, when he astonished Noguchi by bowing deeply and thanking him for coming.

Treatment of asocial juveniles proceeds in three stages, the article explains. Stage One stresses human relationships with designated treatment staff. Stage Two focuses on reconciliation with the parents. Stage Three encourages interaction with a wider variety of individuals.

In the fall of 2000, Noguchi met Sakakibara again, for the first time in two-and-a-half years. "He was not the same boy," he tells the magazine. He was gentle, smiling, and apparently on friendly terms with the staff. He was even seeing his parents, something he had vehemently resisted earlier.

He will probably move back into society via a private government-licensed halfway house, like one in Tokyo *Dias* visits whose residents go out to work (mainly for transport companies) and live in dormitories, bound by a curfew but otherwise unrestricted.

Supposing—an iffy supposition—all goes well. Would success ease lingering dissatisfaction? "Because the criminal was a juvenile," comments one Suma Ward resident, "we have been told nothing—not his name, not his motive. What was it all about? What happened back in May 1997? We'll probably never know." (MH)

EDITOR'S NOTE: Now 22, "Seito Sakakibara" was declared rehabilitated in March 2004 by the Kanto Regional Parole Board. For eight months after his release on parole he remained under the board's guidance and supervision. Since January 1, 2005 he has been free, living in an undisclosed location under an assumed identity.

YAKUZA FACE EXTINCTION

Asahi Geino (February 20, 2002)

Life used to be sweet for the yakuza. The pickings from fraud, extortion and gambling were consistently lucrative, while the police usually turned a blind eye to crime, so long as it was organized.

But that all changed in 1993, says *Asahi Geino*. That's when a tough new law aimed at cracking down on organized crime came into effect. It was also, coincidentally, when Japan's lingering recession got underway. Ever since, the nation's vast army of mobsters has seen some of its prime sources of revenue shrink drastically, thanks to newly vigilant cops and an ever-worsening business climate.

Organized crime in Japan used to do serious business. In 1988, the total earnings of all yakuza groups was ¥1.3 trillion. About 80 percent of that money came from illegal activities, the top earner being the trade in illegal drugs. That was followed by gambling, the collection of protection money and the use of intimidation to settle civil disputes, such as car accidents. The remaining 20 percent of yakuza income came from legal activities.

The anti-yakuza law has put a particularly severe squeeze on protection and intimidation rackets, both of which were previously in legal gray zones. "I used to take in ¥300,000 per business, so I would collect ¥2.1 million from the seven places I shook down," says one unnamed crime boss in Tokyo, recalling his once-lucrative protection racket. "But since the law was created, business is down by a half to a third of that."

Even so, he considers himself lucky. He says about 60 percent of other syndicates are collecting nothing at all in the way of protection money.

One commentator, whom the magazine identifies only as a "yakuza watcher," reckons that the recession has had a more devastating effect on the mob than on law-abiding folk. "Yakuza operators are the first to feel the effects of the recession because they are on the fringe of the economy," he says. "Conversely, in the event the economy recovers, the yakuza will be among the last to feel that recovery."

The economic bad times have caused the closure of such establishments as night clubs and video-game parlors, prime targets of the yakuza's protection rackets. All this has caused many individual hoods to fall on truly pathetic hard times. That much was illustrated by the case of a gangster who died after his house caught fire when a candle toppled over. He had been burning candles because his electricity had been cut off.

Some, on the other hand, have actually managed to prosper. A few have joined the IT revolution in a big way, managing pornographic websites and cell phone Internet sites that put prostitutes and their johns in touch with each other.

Other yakuza groups have forged alliances with their counterparts in Russia and China, where they are engaged in activities ranging from drug smuggling to prostitution to crab poaching. So, just as Japan's salaried workforce has already discovered, the yakuza can no longer afford to be complacent. Survival in the 21st century will require some innovative thinking and an ability to quickly adapt to the momentous changes taking place, not just in Japan but throughout the world. (GB)

WRITER PREDICTS OWN DEMISE

Various Magazines (Fall of 2003)

Kabukicho is not the kind of place where common sense gets you very far. Of course, there are places there where you can walk safely; but if you stick out from the crowd, it can turn on you mercilessly. The underworld of this 'special economic zone' is so murky and so deep you never see its bottom.

That was how Satoru Someya—writing under the name Kuragaki Kashiwabara—summarized his impressions of Tokyo's largest adult entertainment zone in *Kabukicho Underground*, a nonfiction book released last July. By his own accounting, he had spent ¥645,760 in 96 establishments, where he had recorded testimonials from 107 individuals.

Someya's book is entertaining, but probably no more revealing than the numerous other works on the shelves that offer an insider's view into the sleazy district of pachinko emporiums, ethnic restaurants, bars, massage parlors and love hotels. Still, the media was left asking: Did the revelations contained in his book get him killed?

In the early hours of September 12, an excited truck driver summoned police after spotting a body floating in Tokyo Bay. Weighed down with chains, the corpse was punctured by no fewer than eight stab wounds, its head so bludgeoned as to make recognition impossible. The body was eventually identified as Someya, and his death, the autopsy indicated, had occurred elsewhere, between one to two weeks before.

The freelance writer, age 38 at the time of his death, had last been heard from by cell phone on the night of September 5. The following morning, his bag was found on the street in Minami Ikebukuro.

According to *Shukan Post*, Someya was an energetic wordsmith who had covered the Paris-Dakar auto rally and who, in addition to English, was said to be able to converse in French and Chinese. Following his investigative forays into the Shinjuku underworld, he was reputed to have swapped his notes on gangs' drug-dealing and gun-running activities with police, which is why that magazine clings to the theory that Chinese or Korean hoods were behind his demise.

But Kabukicho street guide Li Xiao-mu, himself author of a book on the area's nightlife, disagrees. "Actually, Someya's book was rather superficial," he tells *Shukan Asahi*. "I asked a Chinese gang leader if he had heard anything about the killing; he said he wasn't even aware of Someya's existence."

In any event, the killing of an investigative journalist in Japan is rare enough to move the Tokyo Metropolitan Police to assign a 60-man task force to the case. And there seems to be no lack of suspects, thanks to a number of recent troubles.

Last May, five months in arrears on his rent payments, he had fled his apartment, leaving his guarantor responsible to make good on about ¥500,000 owed to the landlord. "A month earlier, someone had scrawled the message, 'You can't run from us,' on his apartment door," a building resident tells *Shukan Asahi*. "Inside there was broken window glass all over, and ashtrays and candy boxes had been overturned and scattered."

So then—whodunit? The foreign hoods, or the debt collectors? *Sunday Mainichi* suggests another, even more intriguing possibility. According to a gang member who knew Someya, the slain reporter had inside information about an unsolved murder involving a group of S&M enthusiasts that occurred several years ago. Most suspiciously, the unusual technique used to shackle the chains around Someya's corpse was said to be identical to that used by the perpetrator of the earlier murder.

"Writing about the underworld can get pretty hairy sometimes," shrugs author Akira Hinago. "You worry you might be snatched or held hostage. But Japanese gangsters typically try to warn you off first, and it looks like Someya was killed without any preliminaries. Maybe foreigners were involved, but his book didn't single out any particular individuals. I can't see any connection."

If anything's certain at all, concludes *Sunday Mainichi*, form has followed art. Through acts by a person or persons still unknown, Satoru Someya was swallowed into the same bottomless underground he so faithfully described in his book. (MS)

THEY SAID IT IN THE *Weeklies*

"In olden times, it was fairly common for yakuza or profligate gamblers to hire their wives out to brothels. More recently, in households where the main breadwinner has been laid off, it's not unusual for wives to engage in prostitution to help support their family."

—Chuya Nakao, a writer covering the "pink" trade, in *Shukan Asahi* (June 7, 2002) on married women and their husbands—also called *ristora himo*, or "down-sized pimps"

PHONE SCAM MAKES BILLIONS

Shukan Taishu (February 23, 2004)

"Mom? It's me, Yuto. Listen, I'm in trouble..."

"What? What is it?" The mother was frantic. There were strange voices in the background.

"Gimme the phone," said a gruff voice. "Mrs. Yamamoto?"

"Yes..."

"Your son doesn't pay his debts, did you know that? You know what happens to people who don't pay their debts? If you want your son freed, deposit ¥2 million into... Do you have a pencil?" The bank information followed.

Mrs. Yamamoto hung up and, with trembling fingers, dialed Yuto's cell phone number. The number was out of service. This was serious. Hesitation could be fatal. She dashed to the bank to make the transaction demanded of her.

She should have known better—the so-called *"ore-ore"* ("It's me") fraud had been in the news for months—but cool, rational judgment, always easy to prescribe, is less easy to exercise when you think your child's life is in danger. And, as *Shukan Taishu* shows, the scam artists keep getting cleverer and cleverer. The best of them are good actors, and they do their homework.

Yuto's "kidnappers," for example, must have had connections in the shady consumer-loan business to know something of the young man's spending habits. They also knew his cell phone number. Before calling Mrs. Yamamoto they took the precaution of canceling his phone contract.

Telephone fraud of this sort is proliferating at an astonishing rate. National Police Agency statistics show 6,504 reported incidents in 2003, 4,419 of them successful, netting their perpetrators a total of ¥4.3 billion. Only 78 arrests were made.

Arrests are difficult, a police spokesman explains. The bank accounts are prepared in advance under false names. The cell phones used to contact victims are mostly prepaid and untraceable.

"Ore-ore" has a long history—15 years at least, says *Shukan Taishu*. Back then, a classic case went something like this:

A man calls a snack bar. "*Ore da, ore da yo*. It's me, I was there last night, don't you remember?"

"Kawaguchi-san?"

"Right, Kawaguchi. Listen, I'm at this party. Admission is ¥15,000 a head, only I seem to have forgotten my wallet. If I send my brother-in-law over, could you lend him the money? I'll drop by later tonight and pay you back."

More recently, the trick has been to prey on the elderly. Perpetrators scan the phone book for old-fashioned names. They dial the number and talk fast, counting on confusion at the other end. "*Ore da, ore da yo*. It's me, your grandson. Listen, I was in an accident . . ."

Publicity having rendered that approach obsolete, criminal artistry has risen to the occasion.

"Dad? It's me, Kazuhiko." Kazuhiko's dad is 65; Kazuhiko, 45, is his eldest son. "Dad, listen, if I don't pay my debts they'll . . . they'll take me to North Korea!"

"That's right," said a stranger in a grim voice. "If the money isn't in our account by 12, we'll sell your son to the North Koreans."

If you stop and think about it, muses *Shukan Taishu*, it's a pretty unlikely story, "but such is the terror evoked by North Korea that Kazuhiko's father didn't stop and think"—a lapse which cost him ¥3.5 million. (MH)

MOM STRANGLES SON OVER SCHOOL

Friday (April 30, 2004)

All it took was a tad of reluctance from a little second grader to attend more night-time classes after a hard day at school to turn an apparently ideal mother into a demon who killed with her bare hands.

Chiaki Onodera, a 37-year-old housewife widely held in high esteem for her apparently superior parenting skills, was arrested for the murder of her seven-year-old son, Josuke, allegedly strangling him because he refused to attend cram school.

"Just before it happened, we met Chiaki, who was walking around with Josuke and his elder sister. They'd just been playing down near the Tama River. I can't believe how a family that appeared to be so close could've been caught up in an incident like this," a neighbor of the Onoderas tells *Friday*.

Onodera's arrest came on April 6 after she called the police and admitted to throttling her son with her bare hands and a belt in their Kawasaki home. Josuke's sister, also an elementary school pupil, was apparently in the room next door playing a video game as her mother purportedly killed the baby of the Onodera family.

Japan is in the grip of a wave of child abuse cases, the Onodera killing being just one of the latest examples. However, few expected Chiaki Onodera to fall into the trap of taking out her frustrations on her children, especially as those who knew her lauded her for the way she handled kids.

"About a year ago, Josuke and my kid were playing in a park. I took my eyes off them for a second and, when I looked up again, my boy had fallen. Onodera-san was there in an instant, helping out with my boy's cuts," a neighbor says. "The idea that somebody who was so nice to kids could have become embroiled in child abuse is almost unthinkable."

Perhaps not, as a parent of another of Josuke's classmates attests. "It only happened sometimes, but I would see her and think she was suffering from some sort of mental illness," a housewife says. "Just the other day, we had a parent teacher meeting. Onodera-san didn't say a word, just standing there alone with a blank face and staring into the distance. She was always the quiet type, though, and I didn't think she had anything worrying her that much."

But there were signs Onodera was about to crack, such as her refusal to attend a party celebrating the marriage of Josuke's kindergarten teacher on the day before the killing. Relatives also knew she was under strain. "Chiaki really did adore Josuke," one family member tells *Friday*. "But, once he started going to school, I wouldn't say he became rebellious, but he wouldn't do as he was told and she had been worried sick by that." (RC)

HUMANS CLONED BY CON ARTISTS

Shincho 45 (June, 2004)

"I cloned a human," mutters the gaunt, dark-complexioned man in his 50s, who goes by the nickname "Zamacho" (a contraction of *buzama na shacho*, "slovenly company president").

The slob in question was not referring to the latest breakthroughs in genetic science, but to his supposed "creation" of an adopted son, a nonexistent person created by exploiting loopholes in the family registry system.

The "cloner" pulled this off by obtaining copies of the registration papers of several families he knew had arranged to "disappear" to evade debts. Pretending to be acting on behalf of the families, he then filed papers that allowed a person from one of the families to adopt a person from another "disappeared" family. The "adoptee's" family name was then changed and thus a fictional person was created.

This identity is then sold. Armed with a new name and address, the "cloned" person can then apply for national health insurance and can gradually flesh out his new identity, which includes a clean credit history.

Writing in *Shincho 45*, Fumiya Ichihashi, nom de plume of one of Japan's top investigative journalists, describes the variety of ways these spurious identities can be put to use. To a person on a credit blacklist, for example, the new identity enables loans from consumer-credit firms. The "clone" can even propagate new members of his "family" who can borrow more. Finance companies, through exhaustive background checks, can eventually spot the phonies, but considering the expense of a full investigation, it's barely worth a company's while unless the amount of the loan is above ¥1 million.

Despite authorities' efforts to eliminate the loopholes from the family registration process that have allowed the likes of Zamacho to flourish, he and his fellow con-artists have generated phony identities that have swindled businesses out of hundreds of millions of yen.

Cloning is not the first of Zamacho's capers. He turned to a life of paper-crime four years ago, after being laid off from his job as an administration manager in a small steel-trading firm. First he started as a *koza-ya* (bank-account broker), placing ads in tabloid newspapers offering to buy and sell bank accounts, which he purchased from cash-desperate housewives or homeless men at ¥10,000 and up, and sold for about twice that price—or considerably more if the account permitted transactions via the Internet. Such anonymous, untraceable accounts are favored by mail-order swindlers or even kidnappers, who can use them to receive ransom payments.

After a successful run, Zamacho's next step was to shift to low-risk, high-return operations, such as dealing in false IDs that could be used to apply for Japanese passports, at up to ¥500,000 each.

Armed with such passports, men were recruited to travel abroad and conclude marriages with foreign women, or their backers, who pay generous sums. By obtaining a spouse visa these women are then able to enter Japan, possibly to take up lucrative employment in the sex industry. These "husbands" split the proceeds with the broker. The practice appears widespread: about one out of three of the Chinese hostesses apprehended during three months of police roundups in Shinjuku's Kabukicho last year entered Japan by means of such illegal marriage transactions.

In *Shincho 45*, Ichihashi alleges that illegal brokers like Zamacho made it possible for foreign gang leaders to establish a safe base in

Japan. Here, they hire Chinese "students" for criminal activities. For example, he alleges, "students" have committed grisly slayings of entire Japanese families in the town of Haguro, Yamagata Prefecture in April 2001 and Fukuoka City in June 2003.

"After I was laid off, I sort of got into this business by the seat of my pants, just watching what other people were doing," Zamacho tells the writer. "I guess I've done pretty well for a poor ex-salaryman." Still, he tries not to dwell too much about the consequences of his illegal activities. "It scares me half to death," he admits. (MS)

THEY SAID IT IN THE *Weeklies*

"Japanese pronunciation differs from Chinese or English in that speakers do not aspirate droplets of saliva. That can be considered one of the reasons for the reduced possibility of transmission."

—Sakae Inouye of Otsuma Women's University to *Shukan Asahi*, about why Japan, with so many tourists visiting China, did not suffer a single outbreak of SARS (November 14, 2003)

END OF WORLD FOUND IN TOKYO

Various magazines (Summer 2004)

Fin del mundo—the end of the world—is the name Colombian streetwalkers have given to the area around Shin-Okubo station where they ply their trade. The area has a long history as a seedy hangout for hookers, who take their johns to sordid "love hotels" lining the back streets. Through tacit agreement with the girls, the hotels look the other way; after all, they're paid for two hours' tenancy, even though the rooms are typically vacated within 40 minutes.

A census of one section of the area found that households headed by foreign nationals outnumber Japanese 1,929 to 1,577—a remarkable ratio in a country where noncitizens constitute only about 1.5 percent of the total population. But that's only part of the story: The whole district's 7,200 legally registered foreigners may be eclipsed by as many as five times that number of illegals.

"Nobody comes to live here because they like it," a Korean resident tells *Shukan Bunshun*. "It's a lousy environment—noisy until late at night. Rents are higher too; foreigners get charged a premium."

The visit to Shin-Okubo's "Asian Lawless Street" is one of seven articles in the magazine under the heading, "The collapse of law and order in the capital." Ranging from accounts of the half-Malaysian junior high school girl—who on June 22 pushed a 5-year-old Chinese boy off a fifth-story veranda—to a Sri Lankan man allegedly involved in the strangulation murder of a 16-year-old high-school girl in Ibaraki Prefecture, all but one of the seven concerns foreigners.

Shukan Taishu limits its coverage of the foreign-crime problem to just one—the activities of so-called "Arrirang" pickpocket teams from South Korea, some 100 of whom, according to journalist Yasuo Yamamoto, are believed to be operating in Tokyo at any given time. Police suspect they accounted for 917 offences in 2002 and 1,145 last year. A member of one team was shot by a patrolman on June 24 while fleeing from the attempted robbery of an 80-year-old woman in Tokyo's upscale Denenchofu area.

One incentive to thieves from abroad is the awareness that if apprehended, relatively lenient treatment awaits. "In Japan, convicted robbers may serve as little as one year in prison," notes Hiroshi Itakura, professor of Criminal Law at Chuo University. "For first-time offenders, suspended sentences are not unusual."

Despite these disruptions to Japan's domestic tranquility, *Shukan Bunshun* reminds readers that, as opposed to 4.63 million foreigners entering Japan last year, some 20,000 were prosecuted for crimes—which by simple calculation works out as 0.0043 percent crimes per person. Common sense would suggest that such a low figure is reassuring; but, in fact, the magazine concedes, these crimes have seriously shaken local citizens' sense of security.

What's more, asserts author-journalist Hiroshi Kubo in the monthly *Shokun*, these crimes by foreigners constitute a tremendous burden on the fiscal budget. From the initial arrest to incarceration, foreigners charged with violating the Criminal Code must be provided with interpreters and represented by public defenders. They must be housed and fed, sometimes with special foods to accommodate their religious beliefs. Kubo calculates the total cost at ¥13 billion. This does not include salaries for new police and immigration officials (13,374 in 2004 alone) and new jails to house the soaring number of violators, of which foreigners, particularly women, constitute an increasing percentage.

As a partial solution to relieving this burden, Kubo urges Japan to conclude reciprocal treaties with China (the source of 45 percent of crimes by non-resident foreigners) and other Asian countries so that convicted criminals can be repatriated to serve terms at penal institutions in their own countries.

While a growing number of volunteer watch groups have been successful in curbing crime in many Tokyo neighborhoods, *Yomiuri Weekly* notes their ways and means sometimes clash with commercial interests. Last March, merchants and residents in Roppongi, Minato Ward, organized a public safety association; but plans to install surveillance cameras on the street seem to be encountering some resistance.

"If efforts to discourage crime attract too much attention, customers might get the impression this place is unsafe, and not come," frets an unnamed director of the Roppongi Business Promotion Association. (MS)

THEY SAID IT IN THE *Weeklies*

"There are several heroin smuggling syndicates: one made up of Chinese with Malaysian passports, and the other is Nigerians with Western citizenship. Recently, a Canadian route opened, run by a Chinese triad that shifted to Canada before Hong Kong was returned to China in 1997. They deal mainly in extacy and speed."

—A Roppongi night club employee to *Weekly Playboy* (July 6, 2004)

FETISHISTIC BOOTY FILLS THIEF'S HOME

Shukan Jitsuwa (October 11, 2004)

With it being de riguer in Japan for kindergarten kids to wear smocks, schoolboys to be decked out in Prussian military uniforms, schoolgirls to be clad in sailor suits, dowdy dresses for office ladies and drab suits for salarymen, there's no doubt this country has a thing for uniforms. Some Japanese, however, take this national obsession for homogenized outfits a little too far, as *Shukan Jitsuwa* notes.

Kenji Hishida is now awaiting trial for burglary after he was allegedly caught trying to rob a West Japan Railway Co. dormitory in Akashi, Hyogo Prefecture, on September 6. Hishida, however, ignored the wallets, cash and other valuables ripe for the taking at the employees' housing area, instead aiming for a couple of pairs of pants.

Cops suspecting the unemployed 39-year-old's actions were a one-off got a rude shock when they raided his home in the wake of his arrest. "Hishida's place was packed full of every type of uniform imagineable. When investigators asked where he got them from, the suspect freely admitted to stealing them all," a local reporter covering the case tells the magazine. "Nearly everything he'd stolen was a uniform, but there was other stuff, too, like helmets adorned with company logos. Even then, the sheer amount of stuff he'd pinched was incredible. Altogether, there were about 10,000 stolen uniform-related items in his home." The apartment was so crammed, the only available space in the place was a couple of square meters he'd left open on the floor so that he'd have somewhere to sleep.

Hishida had a thing for uniforms for some time. Police say he told them he'd spent the past 15 years traveling around Japan picking up uniforms from places like JR, private railway companies and airlines. "He once worked as a security guard for an airline at Kansai International Airport, so he knows a little bit about how the security business works, and this helped him find a way into companies' facilities and gave him hints about where he could find uniforms inside there," the Hyogo hack says. "He had no urge to take advantage of the demand for these goods in online auction sites and kept everything he stole in his room."

In Hishida's apartment, police found filled with uniforms 80 large cardboard boxes and 10 bags usually reserved for storing futon. They needed a two-ton truck just to carry all the booty seized as evidence.

Hishida, meanwhile, has admitted that he used to spend his time changing in and out of the uniforms, gazing at himself in a mirror and satisfying his fetish. His urges are shared by large numbers, if not always acted on with such feverishness, presenting companies like JR West with plenty of headaches.

"We supply our workers with uniforms, so it's impossible to put a price on them. But they're nothing special, pretty much the same gear as the average laborer would wear," a spokesman for JR West tells *Shukan Jitsuwa*. "It's a good thing he didn't steal the trousers. If he got away with it and had worn the pants, he could have sneaked into a station or onto the tracks and possibly have caused an accident. Then we would have been in real trouble." (RC)

SUICIDE SEEKER FINDS RAPE INSTEAD

Shukan Bunshun (November 4, 2004)

"It was horrible . . . humiliating . . ."

Yui wanted to die. She had slashed her wrist, had hanged herself —to no avail. At her wits' end, she checked into a Net suicide site. On the site's bulletin board she posted a message. Would anyone, she inquired, like to join a despairing high-school girl in death?

One reply, says *Shukan Bunshun*, came from a 45-year-old company employee who seemed no less intent on dying than Yui. He would provide everything necessary, he said—car, sleeping pills, charcoal for carbon monoxide. When they met at Tokyo Station he turned out to be short, pudgy and bald. But what difference did that make?

They drove to a secluded mountain road, had a few drinks, and the man passed Yui the pills. Well, she thought, this is it.

But it wasn't. The bald, pudgy salaryman had something quite different in mind. Groggy, disoriented, Yui was dimly aware of him removing his clothes, then removing hers, then raping her. Her strength gone, resistance was out of the question.

"The next thing I know," she tells the magazine, "I'm standing at a bus stop somewhere, the man and the car nowhere in sight."

What could she do—go to the police? A fine story she would have for them! She still plans to die, she says, but intends from now on to give suicide sites a wide berth.

Shukan Bunshun provides no figures, but its anecdotal evidence suggests that sexual predation of this peculiarly morbid sort is not uncommon.

Masami, unemployed and in her 20s, encountered at a suicide site a woman who agreed to die with her. They arranged to meet at Tokyo Station, but when Masami arrived she was accosted instead by three young men.

"The woman is a friend of ours," they said. "Something came up. She couldn't come."

It was all very odd, but they got to talking, went to a coffee shop, proceeded to a bar, and Masami was touched by how well the three seemed to understand her, how deeply they sympathized. When had they slipped sleeping pills into her drink? She didn't know, but when she came to she found herself being gang-raped. Mercifully she passed out again. Some time later she woke up, bruised and freezing, on a street near Shinjuku Station.

Not long afterward, Masami swallowed an overdose of sleeping pills. She survived.

"Sex crimes of this nature have generally been associated with *deaikei* (encounter) sites," *Shukan Bunshun* hears from a journalist. "But lately the deaikei sites are being more closely regulated"— forcing sexual prowlers to look elsewhere for vulnerable victims. And who is more vulnerable than a would-be suicide afraid to die alone?

A man calling himself Iwao is a familiar figure at suicide sites. The magazine hears about him from Mr. A, a man in his 30s who, with three failed suicides in his background, has turned to informal counseling.

"This guy Iwao," says Mr. A, "left messages on several suicide-site bulletin boards: 'Nagoya man, 51, seeks someone to die with. By hanging. Shall we die contentedly together?' The fact that he's old enough to be their father inspires confidence, and he seems to be a good listener."

He is also clever. Mr. A claims to know of two suicidal high-school girls raped by Iwao; in both cases he was careful to remove all traces of himself from his victims' cell phones. One of the girls sought counseling from Mr. A. But there's only so much a counselor can do. Soon after her brush with Iwao, she killed herself with another man.

"I haven't seen Iwao around lately," Mr. A says. "He's probably still out there, though, doing the same thing under a different name." (MH)

YAKUZA STAR
IN VICTIM ROLE

Asahi Geino (December 9, 2004)

On the holiday weekend of October 9, 32-year-old Masatoshi Yasuoka, employee of a foodstuffs manufacturer, was driving his Toyota minivan along National Highway 357. "It was just before three P.M.," Yasuoka relates to *Asahi Geino*. "Suddenly a man hopped out from between two parked cars on the side of the road and stuck out his arm, which made an audible contact with my rear-view mirror."

The man was an *atari-ya*, a professional accident victim skilled at making contact with moving vehicles appear much worse than they really are. Alighting from his van, a worried Yasuoka approached the man, and asked, "Are you all right?" The man made sounds to indicate he was in extreme pain, but held his arm against his chest to prevent Yasuoka from viewing the extent of the injury. Then the man began cursing Yasuoka's inattentive driving.

"Don't you know pedestrians automatically have the right of way? If I call the police, you'll be prosecuted for violation of the Traffic Control Law." The man then exclaimed that since it was his good right arm, he'd be unable to work at his construction job until it healed.

Yasuoka offered to drive the man to a hospital and then report the accident to the police. The man refused. "I don't have so much free time to waste. Who's going to look after my three kids now? You should be a little more sympathetic toward a victim!"

After an hour and a half of persistent argument, Yasuoka—whose fiancee accompanied him in the car—came to the realization that the only way to rid himself of the nuisance would be to "settle out of court." After a trip to a convenience store ATM, he reluctantly handed over ¥100,000—half the amount the man initially demanded to keep quiet.

Based on the man's name and other information obtained from Yasuoka, *Asahi Geino*'s reporter traced the atari-ya to his home in Tokyo's Katsushika Ward. He discovered the man was an experienced pro with a long record of arrests, and who had only been released from prison about 18 months previously. After his release he worked briefly in the construction trade, but soon gravitated to his former "profession."

Highway 357 is said to be so notorious for these kinds of mishaps, local drivers refer to it as the "Atari-ya Ginza." And since many drivers headed toward Tokyo Disneyland are likely to have children on-board, con artists know they would be more inclined to settle up on the spot than risk spoiling a family outing.

Nor is this the only type of hazard lurking in the vicinity. "A gang-connected group operating in Urayasu City (where Disneyland is located) keeps an eye peeled for license plates from distant prefectures," says a local source. "After hemming them in, the car in front will brake suddenly, causing the target's car to stop; then the one behind will crash into him and the shakedown begins."

To counter these crooks, *Asahi Geino* advises drivers to always keep an instant camera on hand to photograph scenes of the accident—a sensible precaution in any case. And if confronted by a shakedown artist, they should shout to a passing driver or eyewitness to immediately summon the police. Officers, while often slow to proceed to ordinary traffic accidents, tend to respond rapidly to reports of felonious assault. The threat of police intervention alone should be sufficient to make any con artist beat a hasty retreat. (MS)

"PUNISHER"
NOT JUST SCREEN ROLE

Shukan Jitsuwa (December 9, 2004)

A popular TV drama from the 1970s, *"Hissatsu Shiokinin* (Sure-kill Punisher)"* was about an agent in the Edo Period whose job was to exact revenge for his clients. The kimono-clad "punisher" would work on behalf of those who had been slighted, hurt or double-crossed and had then demanded retribution. The revenge was often brutal and merciless.

But while the show may have contained a large dose of historical fantasy, shiokinin are, in fact, a modern-day reality, according to *Shukan Jitsuwa*. That much was learned in the wake of the arrest of Yuji Kato, a private detective based in Nara Prefecture.

Kato is accused of fraud, but investigators and the media have since learned that Kato operated an agency specializing in the business of "punishing" people on behalf of his clients. He reportedly billed himself on his own website as a "contracted agent specializing in revenge."

"The site was set up about three years ago, and he had been approached by dozens of clients throughout the country," a reporter tells the magazine. "He originally started out as a detective, but it seemed he could make more money as a punisher."

The police arrested Kato not because of his supposedly malicious activities, but rather on suspicion of bilking some of his clients. In one of the cases, he was hired by a Tokyo woman to publicize supposed wrongdoing carried out by a social-welfare office. She allegedly hired Kato to place an article in a weekly news magazine detailing the office's improprieties. He is suspected of defrauding the woman of ¥560,000 in fees, which he said were needed to get the article published.

His internet site includes several general areas of the types of revenge he was willing to exact: ruining wedding engagements, ending extramarital affairs or marriages, wreaking revenge on lovers and interfering in certain people's social lives. "Clients would pay ¥100,000 up front and another ¥100,000 in the event of success," says the reporter.

An inordinate number of Kato's revenge-seeking clients were young women. "Lots of the cases were over love-related problems," says a source close to the investigation. It goes on to describe a female office worker in her twenties who enlisted Kato to phone a wedding hall and tell the staff a bomb is planted there. "All she wanted to do was disrupt the wedding ceremony of her former boyfriend who had dumped her," says the source.

In another typical case, a woman having an affair with her boss wanted to pressure the man into a speedy divorce. She asked Kato to abduct the couple's children. The magazine doesn't say whether the punisher accepted the job.

But then Kato, if available for comment, would tell us that none of this should come as a shock. As his website stated: "It's a natural emotion to feel malice and hatred toward individuals who have trampled on your life." (GB)

COPS LOOK ON WHILE YAKUZA KILL

Yomiuri Weekly (January 9, 2005)

Kuniaki Uranaka was a bookish postgraduate student with a sense of righteousness that enabled him to fearlessly take on even the toughest yakuza. Unfortunately for Uranaka, even the finest vanguard of the Hyogo Prefectural Police couldn't collectively muster the same cojones as he had shown, according to *Yomiuri Weekly*. The Kobe District Court confirmed it last month when it ruled his death had been the result of law enforcers' *mikoroshi*, a delightful Japanese word meaning "to stand idly by while another dies."

Uranaka died on March 3, 2002, after he and a 34-year-old male friend became embroiled in a bitter brawl with a yakuza gang boss following a long-running spat over a car parking space. Uranaka and his friend had initially held the upper hand until carloads of the yakuza's cronies arrived on the scene and started pummeling them.

Uranaka had run from the brawl to seek help from officers in his local police box, only to find that they were all napping. When he returned to the scene of the fight, mobsters swarmed over him, beat him senseless and shoved him, unconscious, into one of their cars.

Alerted by local residents, a force of 18 police officers arrived on the scene. Uranaka's friend saw the policemen as saviors, and jumped into what he assumed was the safety of a patrol car. Gangsters grabbed the patrol car door and tried to forcibly open it, while officers did nothing to stop them. Luckily, he was able to fend them off.

One of the yakuza told the ranking police officer that the gangsters would show up later at a police box to explain what had happened, and asked if, for the meantime, the law enforcers would mind leaving the scene. Incredibly, police complied with the request, departing the scene with the battered Uranaka still being held in one of the gangster's vehicles.

"It was bizarre," a man who witnessed the police withdrawal tells *Yomiuri Weekly*. "The cops just stood there doing nothing while they were surrounded by a group of yakuza."

Uranaka's bloodied friend told the officers who drove off in the patrol car where he had sought sanctuary that he believed the 27-year-old postgrad student was still in the gangsters' hands. None of the officers even asked the gangsters about Uranaka.

Soon after the incident, Hyogo Prefectural Police admitted its handling of the case had been a shambles and offered Uranaka's bereaved relatives a formal apology. Several gangsters involved in the case, including the gang boss, have been convicted, with jail terms handed out ranging from 10 to 20 years.

But police remorse over the case apparently lasted only until Uranaka's mother took them and the gangsters to the Kobe District Court in a civil case, accusing them of causing her son's wrongful death. "We thought it was merely a little fight," *Yomiuri Weekly* quotes a police lawyer saying during the case. "We didn't notice Uranaka. We thought he'd got away."

A recording of one of the impassioned pleas for help Uranaka had made in his visits to the police box convinced judges otherwise. "It was clear he faced the danger of being dragged away and beaten, with death easily a foreseeable outcome," the weekly quotes Presiding Judge Yasuyuki Muraoka saying as he awarded the case in favor of Uranaka's grieving, 61-year-old mother.

The mother, who spoke of a studious, kind boy with whom she had lived alone, was pleased with the outcome. "I didn't want the case to be written off as simply a brawl between a bunch of drunks," she tells *Yomiuri Weekly*. "If the police had done their job properly, my son would never have died." (RC)

OUTLAW HOT-RODDERS HIT THE BRAKES

Shukan Taishu (February 21, 2005)

They've been known to cause havoc and terror, not just on the highways and roads but in suburban neighborhoods, beaches and parks throughout the nation. They arrive by the dozens, dressed in combat gear and waving flags and sometimes even swords. Their hopped-up vehicles scream an ear-piercing 120 decibels or more.

These are the *bosozoku*, Japan's version of hot-rodder gangs. Their favorite activities are jamming up the highways and roads, while creating as much noise as possible from their muffler-less motorbikes and cars. Now *Shukan Taishu* tells us these prime menaces to motorists and infamous taunters of the police appear headed for extinction.

That much is indicated in statistics. The police reportedly put the number of all types of hot-rodders in Japan at 93,438 last year, a 31 percent decrease from two years earlier. As for the number of hardcore gang members, their number is about half of what it was during the early 1980s, when their numbers peaked.

Why the decline? The most obvious reason is the tougher laws governing traffic and anti-organized crime that introduced in the last few years. "Nowadays, all you need to do to get arrested is go out in a big group together," says Kenichiro Iwahashi, author of *Zoku* (tribes), which details the hot-rodding phenomenon. "The police, who now see the ties between the bosoku and organized crime as a big problem, are making serious efforts to crush them."

Those efforts are so serious that they deter a lot of young people from even considering becoming a hot-rodders, notes Ritsu Hioki, who runs the bosozoku-oriented Website "Black Emperor." "The net sweeps by the police target not only the bosozoku but also any kind of modified vehicle. There aren't many people who are willing to put up with the stiff fines, or having their vehicles impounded and driving licenses revoked," he says.

Yet a host of other underlying factors, which have more to do with shifting social trends, is also contributing to the gangs' demise. "The bosozoku is the classic case of a vertically integrated society," explains Hiroyuki Kanezaki, a hot-rodder turned lawyer. "The etiquette is a real drag and orders from superiors are absolute." It's no surprise that 21st century delinquents, with their more individualistic bent, are less willing to put up with such a constricted environment.

The youngsters are also turned off for aesthetic reasons. The bosozoku look—featuring exaggerated pleaded trousers and big-shouldered tunics—fell out of favor as a fashion many years ago. A former hot-rodder says, "The other underground groups are a lot more cool looking; they're the ones attracting the girls."

The gangs' internal organization is under siege as they grapple not only with shrinking membership but a particular dearth of members in their 20s to carry on their havoc-creating traditions. Like Japanese society as a whole, *Shukan Taishu* chuckles, the gangs are graying.

Yet even so, Hioki believes the hot-rodders' demise should not be a cause for celebration among the police and intimidated motorists. "It's like when you spray bug killer. All the cockroaches just flee to the next room," he says.

In other words, the number of delinquent youths in Japan, if anything, is probably on the rise. It's just that they're giving the bosozoku a miss by signing up with other, less conspicuous youth gangs, which have been forced to move even farther underground to avoid the police's stepped up efforts against organized crime. "The number of criminally oriented youth is clearly not on a decline," says Yukihiro Ito, a former hot-rodder and now youth counselor. "But the kids know that if they don't belong to the bosozoku they won't get arrested.

And he adds: "The other gangs now are a lot worse than the bosozoku ever were back in the old days." (GB)

The Other Economy

HOMELESS EVICTED BY BLOSSOM VIEWERS

Shukan Taishu (April 16, 2001)

"Until the blossoms fall, we've got to move somewhere else. We don't want anyone to think we're a nuisance."

With a fatalistic sigh, the speaker, a man in his 60s, gathers up a few humble possessions and trudges off from his alfresco home in Shinjuku Chuo Park, leaving it to the revelers who come for their seasonal *o-hanami* (cherry-blossom viewing).

Shukan Taishu reports it's much the same at Ueno, Hama Detached Palace, Sumida Park and other popular blossom-viewing venues in the metropolitan area. As Tokyoites gather to eat, drink and be merry, the disadvantaged are uprooted for the duration.

Reiko Yasue, a volunteer at the Resource Center for Homeless Human Rights, accuses Tokyo park administrators of stepping up their efforts to drive out the homeless. "They won't admit it openly, but there are moves afoot to use o-hanami as a pretext to drive the homeless out of the parks," Yasue complains.

But while these homeless are forced to relocate, at least some find a way to stay and, apparently, gain a short-term windfall: Not only do partygoers leave behind food and beverages, they also discard their vinyl groundsheets, which the homeless utilize as rain shelters. Still other itinerants have found a way to earn a few thousand yen by occupying a space until partygoers arrive after work.

"And if you approach people just as their party's breaking up and offer to clean up for them, they usually agree," chuckles a Sumida Park resident. "Anyway, by that time they're pretty drunk.

"There's usually a half-finished bottle or two, maybe some rice crackers, and some straw matting or vinyl sheets we can put to use," he continues. "Of course, I doubt if any of the visitors think we're actually part of the cleanup crews."

But alas, even the traditional spring revelers appear to have fallen on hard times. "This year, the salarymen haven't been going wild like they used to," a 50-ish resident of Shinjuku Chuo Park observes. "They don't leave much unconsumed booze. And one group of six only brought along four bags of peanuts to munch on."

A long-term resident of Ueno Park, a man in his 60s, has noticed a similar phenomenon. "About two years ago, we could stake out a space under a tree and visitors would buy us out for a couple of thousand yen. And they'd let us have some food, too," he relates. "I guess it's probably the recession, but they don't do that any more. Now if a bum grabs a spot under a tree, instead of paying him, they complain to the park office."

It looks like it will be some time yet before the homeless can join in the revelry, *Shukan Taishu* concludes. (MS)

THEY SAID IT IN THE *Weeklies*

"At the moment we can produce 200 kilowatts of electricity, which is enough to sustain the energy consumption of about 200 average Chinese households."

—Toshiba spokesman to *Weekly Playboy* about an ambitious project to use pig dung to power electricity generators (February 19, 2002)

PRICELESS ART NOW ATTIC JUNK

Weekly Playboy (April 17, 2001)

During the extravagant days of the Bubble Economy, Japanese companies and individuals snapped up renowned *objets d'art* at premium prices.

Weekly Playboy reports that of the 10 highest prices ever paid out for major works of art at auctions, at least five were for works purchased by Japanese bidders between 1987 and 1990. But today, many of these items are not on display in museums or galleries, but sitting in warehouses beneath protective wrapping as they await disposal to clear the debts of their bankrupt former owners.

Take the example of Ryoei Saito, chairman of Daishowa Paper Co., who in 1990 offered his own property as collateral to acquire two major works: Renoir's *"Le Moulin de la Galette"* (for which he paid ¥10.8 billion) and van Gogh's "Portrait of Dr. Gachet" (¥11.4 billion). Saito supposedly purchased them on behalf of the Shizuoka Prefectural Museum of Art. Soon afterward he threw art lovers into a tizzy by remarking that when he died, the paintings would accompany him to the crematory.

Following the collapse of the bubble, the works declined sharply in value, and such firms as the now defunct Yamaichi Securities, leasing company Orix Corp. and others were obliged to offer their previous acquisitions to overseas auction houses for disposal.

But the fate of others is unclear. One famous work that has vanished from sight is Picasso's "Wedding of Pierette," for which Tomonori Tsurumaki, an auto race entrepreneur, paid ¥7.66 billion in 1989. "Two years later, Tsurumaki was declared bankrupt and the painting went to one of his creditors," an art authority tells *Weekly Playboy*. "No one has seen it since. I know of another work by Picasso that's probably sitting in a bank vault somewhere."

According to a veteran auctioneer, Sumitomo Bank alone holds some 7,000 items with a book value in excess of $6 billion. "During the bubble, Japanese speculated in art items to the tune of ¥2 trillion," says Kiyonori Yamamoto, a broker for international auction houses. "The problem now is that items valued at around ¥1 trillion are being held as collateral or security, and the question is how to get them back into circulation?"

"The works held by Sumitomo are now gradually starting to be sold off," says the operator of a gallery in Tokyo who deals with the banks. "But Fuji Bank has yet to make any moves toward selling at all."

Yamamoto believes that many works are languishing in warehouses operated by major trading groups in the Shibaura district on Tokyo's waterfront. "A while back, I was able to visit a warehouse where some of these works were being held by a bank," says an unnamed broker. "Most of them still bore the wrappings put on by the auction houses.

"They'd been there all these years, and their purchasers never even unwrapped them for a look," he said with a chuckle of irony. (MS)

DEBTORS DO THE MIDNIGHT RUN

Yomiuri Weekly (January 20, 2002)

The two trucks quietly pulled away from the apartment building. In the reflection of his rear-view mirror, driver Sho Hatori took a last look back at his customers: husband on the left, wife and child on the right. It's a sight he still remembers.

The husband had been laid off due to corporate restructuring. Then his investments failed, leaving him tens of millions of yen in debt. Flight would mean abandoning his condominium—no great loss, since its market value had fallen to about half of what he owed the bank. "They wound up getting divorced," recalls Hatori. "They figured it would be hard on the wife and kids to be pursued by bill collectors, so it was better to split up."

Hatori worked as a *yonige-ya* (literally, a fly-by-nighter), a service that specializes in helping people make a quick and quiet getaway—and hopefully a new start somewhere else. Then he turned to writing.

Hatori's book on his exploits led to a hit movie in 1991 titled *Yonige-ya Honpo*, and a sequel. "They call it flying by night, but it was relatively rare for us to do the job after dark," Hatori tells *Yomiuri Weekly*. "In residential neighborhoods, the best time is usually between the rubbish pickup, around 8:30 A.M., and 1 P.M., when moms leave to bring their kids home from kindergarten."

About 10 days before the big move, the household's smaller items are gradually carried away. A truck painted to look like a parcel delivery van is often used for this, since it attracts less notice.

When they first appeared in 1991, the yonige-ya specialized in abetting escapes by people with heavy credit-card debts. The business has since evolved with the times. In 1993, many customers were "Narita [Airport] Divorcees,"—those who sought to undo their marriage immediately following their return from their overseas honeymoon. By 1996–97, people desperate to give stalkers the slip, or women fleeing a violent spouse, fed the business.

Then from 1998 came the so-called *risutora-nige* brought on by corporate restructuring. Soon after the failure of Yamaichi Securities that year, Hatori was consulted by five former employees of the company. Of these, three wound up taking flight.

"You'd think people in our line of work would be regarded as sleazy," says Hatori. "But the fact is, we come recommended by lawyers and workers at city government offices. In cases involving domestic violence, not only does the city office lend money to assist the victims, but the police also keep an eye on us during the move just in case." Whatever the moral implications, it would appear the yonige business has a promising future. In 2000, approximately 140,000 people declared personal bankruptcy—a threefold increase over the past five years.

From about two cases a year 10 years ago, Hakodate rent-collector Masaharu Harada now encounters such hasty departures at the rate of two a month. "One man, who had been suffering from the after-effects of a stroke, committed suicide," Harada says with a sigh to *Yomiuri Weekly*. "His daughter fled with her boyfriend, and it took me five days to sell off their possessions. My biggest problem, though, was what to do with her bedridden mother."

As might be expected, a successful disappearance doesn't come easy. One client, a woman in her 30s, was pursued by a stalker both at her home and workplace. She changed her residence, but the stalker was easily able to follow her home after she left the office.

"To make a clean getaway," advises Osamu Ota, president of a detective agency, "you've got to be prepared to break ties with everything and everyone you know." (MS)

DEATH COMES TO WAGE SLAVES

Spa! (December 10, 2002)

Takeshi Saito does the work of six people. His boss does the work of 11. They pay the survivor's price: They are all that's left of a 17-person department. Their 15 colleagues were laid off. Compared to them, perhaps, Saito and his boss are lucky.

It's luck wrapped in misery. Saito, a food-company executive, tells *Spa!* he puts in 120 hours of unpaid overtime a month. He's 32 and earns ¥3.7 million a year. He hasn't a minute to himself. He visits 10 clients a day, studying documents and working via cell phone between appointments. Lunch is five minutes, dinner not much more. Back at the office, there are reports to write. His boss, harassed himself, harasses him: "Who feeds you, eh? We do!"

His one pleasure in life, he says, is coming home and seeing his infant son asleep. "I'd love to see him awake"—but he can't imagine it happening anytime soon.

You'd think a recession would slow things down at the office. Not so, says the magazine. On the contrary, employees remaining after restructuring thins their ranks find themselves so overwhelmed they scarcely know whether they're living or dying. Hence the article's title: "Busy to Death."

Polling 311 young corporate executives, the magazine computes the average monthly overtime burden at 34.9 hours. The "busy to death" feeling kicks in, typically, at 76.6 hours. Saito's 120 hours dwarf that, but set no record. A young man in the IT field does 200 hours.

Takeshi Fujita registers 135 hours at his bank, an industry which has known happier days. At 29, with a yearly income of ¥7 million, he feels on the brink of nervous collapse. The morning assembly begins with employees reciting in chorus: "No excessive lending!" Then come two to three hours on the phone, reassuring jittery clients that the bank is sound. "Go talk to them in person!" shouts the boss. And so Fujita sets out, grimly resigned to catching up on his office work at night.

"The worst," he says, "is that you have to keep changing your approach—soft soap for favored clients, stern front for deadbeats. I'm used to being cursed out, but this one client, an older man—we had to terminate his loan. He listened to me in silence and then said, 'No hard feelings, son, I know you're just doing your job.'

"I couldn't hold back my tears. I dream about it at night—when I can get to sleep."

Takenori Suzuki, 37, remembers the travel business when it was human. Now, with recession-sparked price wars generating salary cuts and staff cuts, the travel agent's department has been slashed from six employees to three, and overtime—130 hours a month in his case—goes largely unpaid. His annual salary is ¥4.5 million.

"Office hours are simply mad," he tells *Spa!* "Each of us is on two phones and three terminals simultaneously. And in the middle of it all, some old lady calls up, saying: 'Now let's see, where should I go...'"

Then office hours are over and the real work begins—drawing up tour plans, writing estimates, negotiating with transport companies and hotels. Suzuki's boss died of overwork last year. Suzuki himself has been hospitalized for overwork-related symptoms.

What keeps him going? "Well," he says, "somebody has to do it, or the company would collapse. And sometimes the customer shows gratitude, and your fatigue flies out the window. I guess," he smiles, "I'm sentimental." (MH)

SLACKERS FIND BETTER LIFE

Weekly Playboy (October 7, 2003)

Okubo spends his days slogging away behind a cash register at a supermarket, a job that earns him ¥150,000 a month.

The money may seem barely above minimum wage, but subsistence level it is not. "When people say, 'That must be tough,' I take it as kind of a joke. When you consider that I go to New York every year, it's not all that bad," the 26-year-old tells *Weekly Playboy* with a grin.

When Okubo makes his regular sojourns to the Big Apple, he always splurges on his favorite hobby—collecting vinyl. "Nothing is more fun than buying records in New York. One time I came back with 100," he says. His "real job" is as a nightclub DJ, even though it's his supermarket job that accounts for most of his earnings. "I live in a one-room place with six tatami mats, but half of it is occupied by my records," he says.

According to the magazine, there's an expression for people like Okubo: "U-¥200,000 celebrities." "U" is short for "under" and the ¥200,000, of course, refers to these guys' monthly wages. And "celebrities?" Because Okubo and others like him manage to lead rather glamorous lives, despite their meager income.

These poverty-line celebrities have evolved out of Japan's woeful economy. Wages and job opportunities for young people continue to shrink. Meanwhile, fewer babies are being born. It's a double whammy that seems to spell disaster for the nation's social security system, as in the coming years there won't be enough wage-earning people to give the needed financial support to the burgeoning number of pensioners.

Faced with such a gloomy financial future, many young working people figure that saving for the future is futile. So why not just live for today?

Another 26-year-old, referred to as Mr. S, spends much of the year working as a truck driver. But when winter rolls around, he takes more than the standard New Year's holiday—he takes off the whole season. That way, he can enjoy the love of his life, snowboarding. "The money I save during the warm months is all for the mountains," he says. "By the time I come back down from the mountains, my savings are right down to zero."

For Mr. I, fulfillment comes from an Italian-built Lamborghini Countach, one of the world's fastest and most expensive sports cars. The 32-year-old acquired his exotic beauty about three years ago for about ¥10 million. His salary at the time was ¥170,000 a month. "All my friends said, 'You're crazy!'" he recalls. "For meals, I have two hamburgers a day, enough to keep me completely happy."

That kind of attitude tends to come as a shock to Japan's older generation, known as being among the world's most frugal savers and prudent consumers. "Young people these days have no compunction about using their money in ways that fit their own personal values," says economic analyst Takuro Morinaga. "They are adept at defining their priorities." (GB)

HOMELESS FAMILIES GO TO CAMP

Josei Seven (October 30, 2003)

"Morning," yawns 5-year-old Yumi Kawamoto, rubbing her eyes.

"Good morning," says her mother, Setsuko. "You weren't cold?"

The family of three lives under two vinyl sheets strung together on the bank of Tokyo's Sumida River. Yukio, a 59-year-old former construction worker, has fixed the interior up quite snugly. Cardboard walls partition three tiny rooms—living room, kitchen and bedroom. The pots, pans and furniture—bedding, table, portable gas stove and radio-cassette player—were mostly salvaged from garbage drops.

The family is one of 18 tent-dwelling households in the vicinity—more cheerful than most, *Josei Seven* says, thanks to Yumi, the only child in the neighborhood.

Setsuko, 49, wears an oversized men's tracksuit. She tries to keep herself neat but, thanks to infrequent visits to the public bath, complains of "homeless skin." She's missing two front teeth and has kidney trouble. Still, she won't go to a hospital. "If I do, they'll take my daughter away."

A Health Ministry survey earlier this year put the nationwide homeless population at 25,269. One remarkable finding was the swelling ranks of female homeless—to 749, about three percent of the total. *Josei Seven* says the official figures "dramatically understate" the reality. Many of the women are wives accompanying husbands who are fleeing debt. Very few homeless couples have children with them. Yumi is a rare exception.

She and her family were evicted from their Saitama apartment last November, owing 11 months' rent. Yukio was in despair. In better days, he had earned ¥700,000 a month as a construction worker. But that was 15 years ago. Work dwindled and dwindled, finally disappearing altogether.

"Let's kill ourselves," he said one day.

"I don't want to die!" sobbed little Yumi.

That settled it. The family took to the streets, determined never to split up.

But how long can they continue this way? Why, *Josei Seven* wonders, doesn't Setsuko take Yumi to a shelter while Yukio goes off in search of work? That way, even if he doesn't find anything, they will be eligible for welfare.

"Because," says Setsuko, "once we separate there's no telling whether we'll ever get back together again."

Some women are homeless alone. Kazuko has been for 20-odd years. She figures she's about 70; she isn't sure. She's rather well-dressed, considering, and strangely content with her lot.

As a child she worked in a *ryokan*. She married at 30. Her husband drank. He died in his fifties, leaving her with nothing. "Collect welfare? Why? To do that I'd have to enter a facility. Here"—she indicates her tent at Shinjuku Chuo Park—"I'm free, and with the volunteers bringing food I don't go hungry. In fact," she adds after a moment's reflection, "I'm better off now than I ever was in my life!" (MH)

BIRTH RATE FALLING, ABORTIONS CONTINUE

Sunday Mainichi (July 15, 2001)

The good news: Japan's declining birth rate inched up in 2000. The bad news: The next millennium is 1000 years away. The brief surge due to millennial baby syndrome will have no lasting impact on an increasingly urgent problem, says *Sunday Mainichi*. Worst-case scenarios show Japan's population halving within 100 years.

What factors are involved here? Late marriage, expanded career opportunities for women, expanded birth-control options, a queasy economy, lack of social services . . . add them all up and you get a host of reasons not to have children. All developed countries are going through this—some, Japan among them, more acutely than others.

But when it comes to abortion, the magazine reports, Japan leaves the rest of the developed world behind. Health, Labor and Welfare Ministry statistics show 333,220 abortions in Japan in 1998, a figure second in the world only to India's (521,215). Britain (167,297) is a distant third.

Abortion normally suggests young singles too randy to be careful and sorry afterward, but in Japan, oddly enough, it is housewives who are keeping abortionists the busiest. Nearly one married woman in four has had at least one abortion. Even after Japan's belated legalization in 1999 of low-dose birth-control pills, abortion flourishes. Why?

It's fundamentally a communication problem, *Sunday Mainichi* suggests—but before we jump to conclusions, let's meet two wives who have been there and back. Their experiences are a generation apart, which will give us an insight into how times have changed.

Sachiko, now 51, was 26, employed and the mother of a 1-year-old daughter when she unexpectedly found herself pregnant. Her husband's family ran a small business hotel in Tokyo, and Sachiko was the unpaid staff. "I had to ask my mother-in-law's permission for everything," she recalls. Her husband was no less under the old lady's thumb. The pregnancy addled him altogether. "It's not up to me!" he cried, helpless almost as a matter of right. He lent Sachiko no support when his mother insisted on an abortion. Since then, the couple has had two other children, and though too busy most of the time to give the matter much thought, Sachiko says she still feels guilty, especially when the anniversary of the procedure rolls around in May.

Back then—in 1975—abortion was twice as common as it is now, and Sachiko's was one of about 670,000 performed that year. Though upset, she accepted it as more or less a matter of course. Aya, 34, had more to say on her own behalf when her emergency arose last year, but in the end she too yielded—not to a mother-in-law but to a husband reeling from a temporary layoff followed by a salary cut.

"We should have practiced birth control," Aya admits now. "But we just avoided the dangerous days and figured it'd be okay." Surely they knew better? Yes, she says—but acting on what you know does not necessarily follow from knowing.

The communication problem the magazine discerns lurks beneath the surface of that dilemma. It was obvious in Sachiko's day that sex was easier to do than to talk about, and it remains true even now. Sex talk is uninhibited in the media but not in the bedroom. There is a feeling among couples that birth-control measures strain sexual spontaneity and hobble the flight into fantasy we look for in sexual intercourse.

Linking sex to life's practicalities—How many kids do we want to have? What kind of lives do we want to lead?—lends it a depth that adults (as opposed to teenagers too young to regard sex as anything but recreation) should demand of their experiences. That, plus male acknowledgment (so far not generally forthcoming) that conception and birth control are not just the woman's problem might ease the pressure on Japan's overbusy abortionists. (MH)

SPOILED SPOUSES; DIVORCE RATE SOARS

Shukan Bunshun (July 19, 2001)

The symbol always outlives what it symbolizes, and so it is with weddings—the bride in white symbolizing virginity, the ceremony itself symbolizing "till death do us part."

Life as it's meant to be is one thing. Then there is life as it is. Virginity aside, marriages are, for better or for worse, increasingly ephemeral. According to *Shukan Bunshun,* divorce rates are climbing so steeply you can't help wondering: Why bother? Why not just live together, till mutual exasperation do us part?

Somehow it hasn't come to that yet, and every rainy season sprouts its crop of June brides and grooms, their shiny faces fixed on eternity. No doubt they read the papers like everyone else, and know what they're up against. Yet flush with youthful confidence, they buoyantly defy the odds.

What *are* they up against? The Health, Labor and Welfare Ministry has some numbers for us. Last year, millennial marriages and millennial births were joined on stage by millennial divorces, a record 264,255 nationwide, up 5.5 percent since 1999 and—here's the shocker—32.8 percent since 1995. And though the media tends to focus on divorces taking place soon after the honeymoon and divorce among the elderly, the most marked increases, notes the magazine, were not among very new or very old couples but among those who have lived together four to 10 years.

The simplest reason for this phenomenon is that wives are no longer content, in the name of duty, to take whatever dirt their husbands throw at them. Which is fine—except, *Shukan Bunshun* says, that in casting off their domestic slavery women have jettisoned the most basic sense of responsibility. No longer silent victims, wives have evolved into shrill despots, wielding, among other scepters, the club of divorce.

The husband doesn't know what hit him, as often as not. Consider the case of the Tokyo architect who married a gas station heiress. The professional dignity may have been on one side, but the money was mostly on the other. The wedding ceremony was first class all the way, at the Imperial Hotel. The first years were happy, and then, abruptly, the wife got into her BMW and drove "home"—to mother and father, that is.

"I've had it," she declared when her husband came to inquire. Further probing uncovered the last straw. The architect's employer was the firm founded by his parents, and one day his mother suggested her daughter-in-law might consider learning draftsmanship so she could be of some help with the family business.

It was no use. She was gone and would not be persuaded back. Eventually the divorce papers were signed, and the man, struck before he knew he was under attack, spun into an alcohol-soaked, tear-stained emotional collapse—a not unusual outcome, says the magazine.

For this as for so much else, blame the bubble economy, which spawned probably the most spoiled generation in the nation's history. Denied nothing, children grew up with towering expectations and no resistance to adversity—defined here as a thwarted whim. It is not the sort of background that bodes well for the future of marriage.

There are three types of divorce, explains *Shukan Bunshun*. About 90 percent are type one—the couple agrees on terms and the courts need not get involved. The remaining 10 percent are either mediated by the Family Court or else thrashed out in the Divorce Court. If you must get divorced, you'll probably want to avoid the latter.

The judges tend to be of two kinds, the split between them generally along lines of gender. Male judges, ambitious and driven, are impatient with divorce cases, regarding them as intellectually beneath them. Female judges, for their part, are often characterized by a surprising unworldliness. A divorce lawyer tells the story of a man charged by his wife with infidelity. The panties in his bag, he swore, were a souvenir from a lingerie pub. The panties were packaged, a corroborating factor, but unfortunately for him, the lady judge knew nothing of lingerie pubs, and ruled in favor of the wife. (MH)

THEY SAID IT IN THE *Weeklies*

"Boys about to undergo entrance exams are at greatest risk from incestuous mothers. They want to get their boys into a good school and then into a top company. That's why the women will do anything to combat something that stops their boys from studying."

—Telephone counselor to *Tokudane Saizensen* about the destructive behavior of some mothers who have sex with their sons to keep their minds from wandering (October 9, 2003)

PARASITE COUPLES DRAIN PARENTS DRY

Spa! (February 5, 2002)

"My husband has a solid income," says Yuko Matsumoto, 34, "but I hate the thought of reducing our standard of living. So what else can we do except depend on my folks?"

The couple's BMW was a present. So was their mahogany furniture. They go drinking often, no doubt to forget their troubles, and when their wallets are empty, they know where to fill them. There are, however, limits . "My parents won't give us more than ¥20,000 or ¥30,000 at a time," says Yuko. "¥100,000 a month max."

With parents so happy to give and children so happy to receive, family harmony reigns, bridging the generation gap. Is there anything wrong in this? "Parasite couples," the acerbic term *Spa!* coins to describe the beneficiaries, echoes "parasite singles"—the phenomenon of unmarried people who continue living with, generally off, their parents. Recently, the magazine finds, even marriage, late though it often is, does not necessarily mark the start of independent adult life.

Keika Suzuki, a 26-year-old temp worker, has a 3-year-old daughter she sees once a week. The little girl lives with her grandparents. "My husband and I are busy," says Keika. "It's best for the child"— who sees her father, a 34-year-old trading company employee, once a month. Another faint shadow mars the couple's bustling connubial happiness. He is keen on saving money. She is keen on spending it, mostly on brand-name goods. Fortunately, her mom and dad provide pocket money as well as surrogate parenthood.

Megumi Kato, 26, has a husband and child, neither of which

she wanted, but these things happen. When she got pregnant, her 36-year-old boyfriend talked her out of an abortion. His parents had been after him to marry and give them a grandchild. Here was his chance. "All right," agreed Megumi, "on one condition." The condition amounted almost to ransom. Besides providing the couple a place to live and a ¥150,000 monthly allowance, the grandparents have ended up raising the child by themselves.

Takako Sakai is a 26-year-old housewife, whose husband works for a public corporation. There's no telling what its future is, in these days of reform and restructuring. The nervous couple need a nest egg. "How about," suggested Takako, "moving in with my folks?" That way there's no rent, no furniture to buy, no utility bills to pay, no housework to do. And the couple puts aside ¥70,000 a month.

Marriage is not even a prerequisite for conjugal sponging, *Spa!* finds. Ken Tanikawa is a 26-year-old *freeter* whose odd-job earnings left him chronically short of rent money. So his girlfriend brought him home with her. Things went well at first, but finally her father lost his temper—the young man seemed a little too comfortable in an arrangement the girl's family saw as temporary. "If he leaves," cried the girlfriend, "I'll kill myself!" That shut dad up.

Granted, the economy is shaky, but even so, shouldn't young people be eager, in spite of obstacles, to break free of parental constraints and protection, and forge lives of their own?

Blame the distorted times, *Spa!* is told by sociologist Masaharu Yamada, who first named and studied the "parasite single" phenomenon. Within the lifetime of today's crop of young adults, sudden wealth suddenly evaporated, leaving the threat, if not the actual experience, of poverty. More robust generations knew how to cope with poverty; this one doesn't.

Besides, adds Yamada, "Most parasite singles willingly sacrifice marriage to economic freedom and unlimited consumption. So parents are pushed into saying, 'Marry—we'll support you.'" However well meaning, they unwittingly foster perpetual childhood, an incongruous accompaniment to the rapid aging at the other end of the demographic spectrum. (MH)

THEY SAID IT IN THE *Weeklies*

"All housewives ever do is look after the kids and the housework, so there's very little in their lives that can give them much of a thrill. I needed something to spice up my life."

—36-year-old "homemaker" Yuki to *Shukan Taishu*, about the tattoo of a witch riding a broomstick on her left breast (February 23, 2004)

There is nothing Daisuke won't do for his mother. At 27, he has just put his seal on a 35-year loan to buy her a house.

Well, it's not entirely hers, since Daisuke and his fiancee plan to move in with her one day. Still, this is an expensive gesture.

If the word *mazakon* ("mother complex") springs to mind, that's understandable; post-adolescent affection for parents is all too often treated as a perversity. But, no, the appropriate word in this case, a much pleasanter one, is *oyakoko* (filial piety). Confucian? Yes. Outmoded? Maybe not. *Spa!* heralds "the awakening of the oyakoko mind." A filial piety boom.

Oyakoko comes in two formats—casual and hardcore. Casual is helping mom with the dishes, taking out the garbage, phoning home from time to time. Hardcore is anything from meeting dad regularly for golf to marrying a rich man for the sake of the parental blessing. One 23-year-old man treated his father to four days at an onsen resort. The father had been laid off after 35 years, and his son hoped the vacation would lift his spirits. The pitiless economic decline, hitting the middle-aged hardest, partly explains the resurgence of filial sympathy, *Spa!* says.

Daisuke, a computer company employee, is used to taking financial charge at home. His parents divorced six years ago. Even before that, the family struggled financially and Daisuke worked his way (and his younger sister's) through college. But there's more to it than money. Mom is something of a live wire who needs a little filial supervision, which Daisuke conscientiously provides.

Once, he says, he dropped into a bar his mother was drinking at and found her making an intoxicated if amiable nuisance of herself with actor Beat Takeshi. Apologizing profusely, Daisuke led her away. "Since then," he grins, "I make a point of checking up on her."

Oyakoko, says Daisuke, is a masculine virtue. *Spa!* seems to agree; there are few daughters in its story. "How can I be happy," Daisuke reflects, "knowing someone in my family isn't?"

Filial piety takes odd forms. Meet Yasunori. He's 25, a playboy, not one of the world's workers. In fact, he's unemployed, though not poor. He has a talent for pachinko and parlays it into a steady income, though his parents would be mortified if they knew.

Growing up, he'd never had much to do with his parents. Then, one day a couple of years ago, he tagged along while a girlfriend bought flowers for her mother's birthday. How interesting, he thought—and how grown-up! What a contrast to his scapegrace self, who would never in a million years have thought of such a thing.

That was his oyakoko epiphany. He started dropping in on his parents, taking them out to dinner. He made up a story for their benefit about working at a friend's printing company, and when they seemed skeptical, he brought the friend along to back him up. Meanwhile, he tries harder than ever to keep winning at pachinko, buttressing a fake job with real cash. All in the name of oyakoko!

How pervasive is filial piety today? It's hard to quantify, but if, as *Spa!* claims, it has percolated even into rap music, we may suppose it has spread fairly widely. Rino Latina II, whose first album is selling briskly, may be the world's only rap artist who helps out at his mom's yakitori restaurant. His reasoning is simple: "I wouldn't be here without my parents." It's not a typical rap theme, but not a bad one either. It may be closer to the cutting edge than it sounds.

As sociologist Atsushi Miura says, oyakoko is just the balm that ailing 21st-century Japan needs. (MH)

SNIFFLES TRAGIC FOR SOME LOVE LIVES

Shukan Taishu (April 8, 2002)

Many people know how nasty hay fever can be. Burdened by constantly running noses, sneezing and itchy eyes, life can become a struggle. Add to that the secondary effects of lethargy and reduced powers of concentration, and it seems that even the economy is being affected this hay fever season by the large numbers of afflicted workers.

Now *Shukan Taishu*, in its never-ending attempt to put a sexual spin on the major issues of the day, discovers that hay fever is a scourge of yet another sort: The condition is interfering with the sex lives of a large number of couples.

Hideo Yamanaka, head of the Hibiya Clinic in Tokyo, explains that hay fever plays havoc with the body's mucous membranes, some of which are located in our nether regions. "Our sexual desire is largely influenced by the condition of our mucous membranes," he says. "So when these hay fever symptoms emerge, sex can be a problem for many people. Also, their power of concentration declines and they start avoiding sex."

Mr. B, a department store employee and one of several hay fever sufferers the magazine talks to, describes the day his sexual relationship with his wife ended. "I couldn't stop sneezing and my nose wouldn't stop running . . . I was frequently having to blow my nose in the middle of the action. All my wife could do was wait in silence," he says. "Then, not surprisingly, she burst out angrily, saying 'That's it!' She outright refused to have sex. And ever since . . ."

Another recently celibate victim, a salesman in his 30s, recalls the time a sudden sneezing fit he suffered at a highly inopportune moment nearly caused his wife to choke so badly he thought she was suffocating. "That has left her in a kind of trauma. She has been quiet and aloof ever since," he says.

Of course, there is nothing sexy about a partner who is constantly sneezing and blowing their nose. "My wife's sneezing and sniffing wouldn't stop, and what's more her face was all puffy," grumbles a sales rep in his 40s. "Whenever I thought about it, I just got soft."

For Mr. G, a chronic hay fever victim, the problem is the condition's effect on his mental faculties. "When it happens, my head goes hazy, and the moment I sneeze I forget everything that has happened up until that point," he says.

He nonetheless recalls the night that ended his marital sex life. "I was trying to entice my wife to bed. But then suddenly my consciousness faded and I started blabbering the name of the woman I was having an affair with," he says.

Even so, a few couples have found that hay fever symptoms can actually enhance their sex lives, notably the heightened sexual effect that sneezing has on the mind and body. That is the case with the wife of Mr. H, who is in his 30s and works for an appliance manufacturer.

He explains that whenever his wife sneezes, certain of her muscles suddenly tighten up. "And when she has a series of sneezing fits, it's even better," he boasts. (GB)

SEX HARASSMENT FINDS HOME AT HOME

Sunday Mainichi (May 25, 2003)

Japan is filled with wild claims of sexual harassment, but now it appears the average home is rife with cases of children being treated as sex objects by their older relatives.

"My old man really makes me mad. He keeps asking me whether I'm wearing a bra or if my tits have grown," a junior high schoolgirl tells *Sunday Mainichi*. "And my old lady keeps telling me I'm ugly and my body's no good. She says I'd better learn some skill so that I can find a job."

Though workplaces and schools are taking an increasingly tough line against sexual harassment, little is being done if it occurs in the home. An example from a woman now in her 30s.

"I remember when I was about 12 or 13. I'd be in the bath and Dad would deliberately burst in on me to let me know he'd arrived home from work. He never did that to my brother," she says. "Other times I'd be getting changed in my bedroom and Dad would come in without knocking. He'd pretend he didn't realize I was changing, but even then I knew what he was doing."

Lawyer Yuko Suganuma says that combating sexual harassment in the home is as much a matter of "can't" as "won't." "Unlike the workplace, where sex is not supposed to play a part at all, sexual harassment in the home is not as easy as simply making it illegal for a father to tell his daughter that her breasts have grown. But, except in extreme cases of violence or abuse, dealing with sexual issues in the home has always been a taboo topic," she tells the magazine.

Plenty of women complain of sexual harassment at their fathers' hands. "It annoys the hell out of me that my Dad can sit there watching television, raving 'Cor, look at that bird's tits,' or 'she's a dog, get her off.' He doesn't care what sort of character the woman has, he only judges them by their looks," one woman says.

Most sexual harassment in the home offenders are fathers, with pubescent daughters the most likely victims. Though many fathers may feel they're only taking an interest in watching their beloved daughters grow up, for the girls, having their dad stare at their budding breasts or question them about their periods is apparently a torturous burden.

It's not just fathers who are at wrong in this touchy subject, though. Moms have been known to get out of hand. "Mothers get together and talk in loud voices about whose daughters have started their periods and who haven't," a woman now in her 20s says. "God I hated my mom for that."

And some men have had awful experiences, as one guy now in his 30s recalls. "When I was in junior high school, my mom and older sister used to come into my bedroom every day and wake me up by ripping down my pajama pants and giggling when they saw my morning glory," he says.

Hatsuko Takayanagi, a representative of CAP, a group aimed at protecting children from violence, warns that sexual harassment in the home can have dire consequences. "I think there are probably loads of kids who're suffering terribly because of the way family members treat or talk about sex," she tells *Sunday Mainichi*. "Kids have actually told me about their worries when I've traveled around schools. What may be something only minor in the eyes of an adult can turn out to be something so frightening for a child they're too scared to talk about it to anybody else." (RC)

MOMS MISTAKE KIDS FOR PETS

Shukan Bunshun (July 31, 2003)

Shibuya, Tokyo's fashion core, swarms with preteen girls and their moms. "In my class," says a grade-six girl who came, mom in tow, all the way from Ishikawa Prefecture, "some kids dress from head to toe in brand-name fashions. Some kids aren't interested in fashion at all. They're *dasai*—uncool. Me, I'm sort of in between."

Elementary schools are spawning "fashion hierarchies," says *Shukan Bunshun*, and the struggle for rank within them is sapping energy more profitably expended elsewhere. Moms, the article declares, are as bad as the kids, if not worse. Far from reining in a preoccupation which, in teenagers, may be a harmless frivolity but in preteen children is potentially character-destroying, many moms egg on their daughters. Why? Because, the magazine suspects, they are intent on turning their children into pets.

If so, they draw considerable encouragement from the fashion industry. There's big money involved. Children's clothing represents a trillion-yen-a-year market. As the juvenile population shrinks, the hard-sell gets harder and the prices climb higher. A brand-name T-shirt can cost ¥6,000; a pair of trainers, ¥20,000; a miniskirt, ¥15,000. To balk is to risk paying a price of a different kind—that of seeing your child slip down the "fashion hierarchy."

It's not always a gentle descent. Clothes and accessories can bring out the worst in youngsters. Dasai kids are liable to be bullied because they're unfashionable. Fashionable kids are vulnerable too—for the envy and resentment they arouse.

"What should I wear?" becomes a charged question, an anxiety-fraught perplexity. Preteen magazines, with their sexy clothes, provocative poses and "adult beauty tips," are thumbed feverishly for answers. A recent survey shows 63.1 percent of girls in grades five and six paint their nails, 28.7 percent wear lipstick and 27.8 percent use perfume. *Shukan Bunshun* speaks to a mother whose fifth-grade daughter spends 40 minutes each morning styling her hair. Far from disapproving, the mother is the driving force behind the operation, and gets furious when the girl comes home from school with her hair in disarray.

This is "a twisted form of self-love," the magazine hears from an indignant fashion journalist. But it gets worse. "Most of the elementary school girls who come to me," says a plastic surgeon, "come in obedience to their mothers. When I speak to the child alone and say, 'Do you really want this surgery?,' often enough the reply is a bewildered silence."

The heaviest demand is for folded eyelids. The operation costs about ¥100,000 and is over in minutes. Probably all of us have more or less passing feelings of distaste for our own faces. Should these feelings be encouraged in children too young to think through the implications? How about when the child is four and mom hopes a made-over appearance will help get her into an elite nursery school?

No wonder adolescence is turning increasingly explosive, *Shukan Bunshun* concludes grimly, citing as one example the alleged murder of a Nagasaki four-year-old by a 12-year-old. Children don't fit in pet cages. One way or another, when the time comes, they will break out. (MH)

IDIOTS RAISING SIMILAR OFFSPRING

Shukan Bunshun (April 15, 2004)

Nail polish on infants? Well, why not? "It's so cute!" gush their moms.

"Yes, but it's dangerous, I tell them," fumes a nurse to *Shukan Bunshun*. "Babies put their fingers in their mouths. The mothers don't listen." Cuteness trumps health, and the nail polishing continues. Not only nail polishing—hair dyeing and ear-piercing too. Can you imagine an infant not yet a year old with dyed hair and pierced ears?

The article's headline leaves no doubt as to where the magazine stands: "Idiot parents are destroying their children." Idiot mothers, for the most part. Fathers are barely acknowledged; their role, when they have one, is that of indifferent onlooker. The young parents of today are the children of yesterday's free-wheeling bubble economy. They grew up thinking the pleasures of youth were a lifelong entitlement. Their parents never told them otherwise. They'll have to learn on their own, but so far, they'd rather not.

"We had a 3-year-old child staying with us—she had a fever," says a Kanagawa Prefecture hospital nurse. "Suddenly we lost all contact with the parents. Six days later the mother comes in, all suntanned. 'It seemed like such a good opportunity so my husband and I went to Guam,' she said, passing out souvenirs to the nurses. We just didn't know what to say."

"On parents' day lately," says a Hyogo Prefecture nursery school director, "many of the mothers were totally wrapped up in their cell phones—talking, exchanging mail. We have to get them involved in the children's games, just so they'll pay attention.

"Also," the director continues, "many of them can't read kanji. We have to simplify the notices we send home. Sadly, mothers are reading less and less to their children. The children beg to be read to. 'No!' the mothers snap. 'If you keep bugging me about that, I won't like you any more.'"

"When I ask the children what they had for breakfast," says a nursery school teacher in Fukuoka, "I get answers like, 'a chocolate bar'; 'a *senbei* cracker.'"

A colleague in Ibaraki faces the same problem, and wonders, ironically, if nursery schools aren't wrong to serve natural, nutritious, balanced lunches. "It gives parents an excuse," she explains, "to say, 'They get a good meal at school, so it doesn't matter what they eat at home.'"

Let's drop into a "kids' room" for a moment. The little glassed-in room overflows with small children. Judging by the noise, they are having a pretty good time. There are toys, a slide, a video showing *anime* cartoons. You'd hardly think you're in an *izakaya* pub, but that is where this " kids' room" is. It's an innovation that's catching on, *Shukan Bunshun* finds. It lets the whole family go out on the town.

But small children's appetite for night life is limited. By the time 11 P.M. rolls around, the little ones are tugging at their partying parents' sleeves. "Let's go home," they beg. "Not yet," scowls an impatient mother. "Go play." And the party swings on into the small hours. (MH)

COUPLES SPLIT, REMAIN WHOLE

Sunday Mainichi (July 25, 2004)

On June 23, actors Naoki Hosaka and Saki Takaoka held a news conference to announce their divorce. The marriage foundered, they explained, over "a clash of values." What about the children? queried reporters. There are two, aged six and four.

"Nothing will change," replied Takaoka, "since we'll still be living together."

Still be living together? After the divorce? "That's not unusual in the entertainment world," says a veteran entertainment journalist.

It's not so very unusual in the non-entertainment world either, *Sunday Mainichi* discovers to its surprise. The number of divorces has risen steadily since the 1950s—there were 283,906 in 2003, up 1.4 percent from the previous all-time high in 2001, according to the Health, Labor and Welfare Ministry. As divorce becomes more routine, approaches to it have changed.

"Violent emotions and tragic scenes are things of the past," *Sunday Mainichi* finds. "Today, more and more people are settling their affairs in a calm and collected manner."

When Tetsuo, 49, and Atsuko, 51, divorced on the grounds of Tetsuo's abusive behavior, their son was in his final year of senior high school. Breaking up the household at that critical juncture might have undermined his education. And Atsuko had yet to secure a sufficient income for herself. A year later, with the son safely in university and Atsuko having moved from part-time to full-time employment, the couple parted company—with what relief one can easily imagine.

They had installed locks on the doors to their separate bedrooms. A rope slung diagonally across the living room divided her section of it from his. By agreement, Atsuko and the son had the use of the kitchen from 5:00 P.M. to 9:00 P.M.; Tetsuo had it from 9:30 P.M. to 11:00 P.M. The bath was Atsuko's from 9:00 P.M. to 10:00 P.M., Tetsuo's from 11:00 P.M. to midnight.

It sounds anything but homey, comments the magazine, but Atsuko is satisfied the arrangement served its purpose. "We were able to protect our son's educational environment," she says. "If it had been just him and me, he might have ended up quitting school."

Takako and Noboru, both 38, continue to live together more than three years after their divorce. She works for a company; he, for the government. The marriage broke up over his philandering. There were two small children, one still in nursery school, and ¥30 million owing on a condominium purchased two years before. "Divorce doesn't nullify the housing loan," remarks a divorce counselor. When efforts to sell the condo failed, Takako and Noboru resigned themselves to staying together indefinitely.

They have a rule: In front of the kids, they talk to each other as if they were on normal speaking terms. Absent the children, they communicate, when absolutely necessary, only in writing. Respective financial contributions to household maintenance are in strict proportion to income. Takako declares herself grimly content. "We can give the children better care together than I could living with them as a single mother," she says.

Let's hope the children grow up to be grateful—or better still, that they never learn the awful debt they owe their parents. (MH)

MATERNAL LOVE JUNKIES NEED FIX

Shukan Jitsuwa (October 21, 2004)

Scores of coddled young Japanese men drenched in maternal love are now flooding the Internet with ads begging older women to become their "mommies," according to *Shukan Jitsuwa*. Among those messages floating through cyberspace are many like these examples:

"I'm looking for a mommy in her 40s. I'm a 23-year-old company employee. I've always been spoiled, but young women today are too headstrong and they won't spoil me at all. Would you clean my ears for me as I lay my head on your lap about once every week? I can pay about ¥10,000 a time."

Or,

"I got a job and moved from Aomori to Tokyo in the spring. I've been a bit homesick recently and desperately need a gentle mommy. I don't make much money, so would you be kind enough to look after me for ¥5,000 a time? Please make a meal for me at my apartment and then sleep next to me that night. I have got a girlfriend, but I'm too embarrassed to ask her to do these kinds of things."

More and more Japanese guys are posting messages of this unbelievable ilk. But it's a mutual urge, with lonely middle-aged women flocking to answer the call for cosseting.

Where normal personals from guys are lucky to attract even a single reply, those seeking mommies regularly average 10 answers or more from eager women. "Most women looking to become mommies are in their early 40s with kids who're no longer taking up so much of their time. Housewives in this age group usually have kids who're right in the middle of their teenage rebellion years. That means their husbands are too busy at work and are never at home. If a young guy pops up before them, offering himself, they're bound to jump at the chance," Yukio Murakami, a writer up on Japanese cultural trends on the Internet, tells the magazine. "These women do take money at first, but after a while it often becomes the woman who gives the guy presents. Young guys get even more reason to find mommies more attractive than a relationship with women from their own age group."

Older women are also highly valued for the greater arsenal of sexual techniques they bring to the bedroom, as well as for a more advanced concern for personal hygiene than their younger counterparts. With many younger women not changing their panties for days at a time, older women have become ever more appealing.

As it's common for Japanese mothers to overindulge their precious little boys from birth to well past puberty, even many guys who appear to be mature at work may still have the urge to be "mothered" by an older woman willing to spoil them rotten in their spare time.

"Young men nowadays aren't used to being harmonious with everybody, so they can't adapt to life as a salaryman," cultural commentator Murakami tells *Shukan Jitsuwa*. "When it comes to relationships, they want to expend as little energy as possible. They want women who're going to do even more for them than their own mommies did when they were growing up. They want to take the easy way out, even when it comes to sex or simply talking. I'd say that's what's created this great demand for mommies." (RC)

ZOO CREATURES TOLD TO TAKE HIKE

Yomiuri Weekly (March 17, 2002)

You think we have it bad. Well, we do, of course—this is not an easy economy to live with—but consider another perspective. You're a seal, not as young and graceful as you used to be. Or an elephant whose bulk no longer impresses, or a lion past your roaring prime.

The whole story is in *Yomiuri Weekly*'s headline: "Animal Restructuring. Laid-off Lions; Demoted Hippos." The difference between them and us? We know, more or less, what's hitting us. They don't.

In Shiga Prefecture, there's an establishment called the Horii Zoo, a kind of retirement home, or "warehouse," if you like, for the growing number of animals rendered superfluous by a steadily diminishing interest in zoos. "This sea lion is from an aquarium in Hokkaido," says zookeeper Yoshitomo Horii as he shows the reporter around. "This green monkey is from Hokuriku. The chimp you see over there came to us from Hokkaido." Inmates number in the hundreds, from giraffes, camels and pumas to small animals and birds.

Theirs is no easy retirement. They are crated rather than housed, their confinement tight enough to bring warnings from prefectural inspectors. Horii admits the problem. "I want to get them more space, fast," he says. But he doesn't have it, and who else will take them? Zoos not closing down are cutting back, and have no room for surplus animals. If Horii didn't accommodate them, however inadequately, they would probably have to be put to sleep.

A day at the zoo used to be one of the great pleasures of family life. In 1991, Japan's 167 major zoos and aquariums entertained

61 million visitors. By 2000, the number of visitors had shrunk to 42 million. Why? Fewer kids; easier access to more varied, more graphic entertainment. Lions no longer thrill, tropical birds no longer astonish.

The Takasakiyama Nature Animal Park in Oita, Kyushu, used to draw 1.9 million people a year. Now it gets one-fifth that. Debts and monkeys multiply; gate receipts dwindle. Hokkaido's Kushiro City Zoo calculates its revenues cover one-sixth its expenses. Tokyo's Ueno Zoo saw its annual attendance drop from 7.5 million in 1975 to three million in 2000.

This is sad for the zookeepers; sadder still for the uncomprehending beasts ruminating blankly over their fate at Horii's zoo—what else do they have to do? Think of the place, *Yomiuri Weekly* suggests whimsically, as a re-employment agency, a kind of Hello Work for applicants eager to please but lacking market value. A few may have a future as pets. As for the rest, there is consolation in the fact—the probable fact—that their brutish emotional range does not extend to despair.

There is one more wisp of consolation, perhaps even of hope. When a private railway announced in 1998 the closure of a zoo it was operating in Kitakyushu, 260,000 locals signed a petition in protest. In response, the city purchased the facility and turned it into Itozu Forest Park, set to open in April. (MH)

SPA TREATMENT FOR STRESSED OUT PETS

Yomiuri Weekly (November 3, 2002)

At one aesthetic salon in Tokyo's Setagaya Ward, customers get royal treatment. It starts with a mud pack using mud from the Dead Sea, followed by a massage, shampoo, haircut, manicure and ear-wax removal.

The customers at Pet Salon Jenny's, it should be mentioned, are dogs. And the beauty treatment they receive at the hands of professionals would be the envy of many humans. The full course runs to about ¥15,000 for a small dog, not much different from what a human would pay for the same service at a regular salon.

Yomiuri Weekly suggests that many pets may actually need such therapeutic pampering, as they, like humans, are not immune to the stresses of modern life. Our problems, namely the breakdown of the extended family, the graying of society and work-related stress, can easily rub off on our animal friends.

The cat of a salaryman who lives alone, for instance, is prone to chronic loneliness. The dog of an elderly couple too infirm to take it on long walks no doubt feels a deep sense of frustration.

The pet business recognizes all this, which is why it now offers a wide range of services aimed at relieving the anxieties of our furry companions. "These days, it's important to treat things which Western medicine doesn't cover, such as caring for a pet's spiritual needs," says Keiko Sugimoto, a veterinarian at the Minamikoiwa Pet Clinic in Tokyo's Shinagawa Ward.

For the past six or seven years, Sugimoto has been giving pets a therapeutic treatment using flower essences. The liquid is made from water in which flower petals are soaked, dried and then mixed with brandy. When ingested or massaged into the skin, it purportedly alleviates negative emotional states.

Animals can also enjoy the benefits of medicinal hot springs, thanks to Animayu, a chain of 16 resorts located in the Kanto and Kyushu regions. And for pets suffering from loneliness, there is a surrogate mate in the form of a so-called Companimal. The object may look like nothing more than a furry stuffed dog or cat, but inside is a device that simulates the beat and vibration of the heart. It also has pockets where warmers or milk-feeding bottles can be inserted. The idea is to get lonely or neglected pets to snuggle up to the Companimal while their owners are away.

Expect to see more such therapeutic products and services in the future, says Nobuaki Komori, the director of Anicom, a company pushing health insurance for animals. "There are more and more pet owners who cherish their pets in the same way they would their own children," says Komori, a pet-market analyst. "Even in a recession, it's hard to imagine that businesses based on affection and emotional ties could ever fail." (GB)

DOG'S LIFE
FOR PET POOCHES

Uwasa no Shinso (May, 2003)

"Three years ago, small dogs started getting popular," says the owner of a Tokyo pet shop. "Miniature Dachshunds were in greatest demand by far. Chihuahuas were popular too, but sold maybe one-third as many as the Dachshunds. Then came Aiful's TV commercial, and before you knew it, the positions were reversed."

Writing in the monthly *Uwasa no Shinso*, reporter Yuji Fukuda notes that since Aiful, a *sarakin* (consumer-finance company) scored a hit with a commercial showing a cute Chihuahua clad in a tuxedo, it's become the rage for young women to prance around town with tiny pets poking out from inside their shoulder bags.

Unfortunately for shop owners wishing to exploit this market, supplying the sudden demand hasn't been easy. "Dogs typically produce two litters a year," says the pet-shop owner. "Big breeds, like the Siberian Husky can bear as many as 10 pups per litter. But a Chihuahua might have only one or two.

"We try to put males to work as full-time studs, but the poor little guys poop out in nothing flat," he chuckles. This inability to breed prolifically has led to the price of a pedigreed Chihuahua rising to ¥200,000 or more.

Aside from the money involved, there's a depressing downside to these booms as many owners grow weary of caring for their pets. Packs of feral Huskies, abandoned in rural areas by their owners, have been causing problems for local residents. Animal shelters are full of mournful Golden Retrievers whose owners tired of them. Eventually the dogs must be destroyed.

Unsold pet-shop inventories are dealt with equally callously. "If we can't find any buyers, we might use them for breeding," says the pet-store operator. "But because there's not much likelihood that their offspring will sell well, the only thing left to do is destroy them. Or, they can be sent to laboratories and used for research."

Chihuahuas are said to be favored by bar hostesses and other women working in the "water trade," who live alone and desire a pet for companionship. And if they play their cards right, the dog can also help generate extra income for its owner.

"Actually, a woman will sometimes just borrow the dog from us," says the store owner. "They'll get their sugar daddies to spring for several hundred thousand yen, and then after a couple of days 'forget' to shut the door and let the animal escape. She'll pretend to be so heartbroken at its 'escape' that the patron will fork out more money to buy her a new one. We'll give her the same dog again, and kick back the money." There's little chance the "papas" will catch on to the scam, since dogs, like dead men, tell no tales.

Uwasa no Shinso saves its final salvo for the Japan Kennel Club. Founded as an Agriculture, Forestry and Fisheries Ministry-approved public body in 1949, it is, the magazine alleges, operated for the benefit of those involved in selling the dogs, and accordingly has made little contribution to animal rights.

"One of the JKC's directors, who bills himself as an 'animal essayist,' has never even owned a dog," says the unnamed editor of a pet-enthusiast magazine. "The director of another pet association has authored ghostwritten books in which he bills himself as a veterinarian when he actually runs a pet-grooming salon. The fact is, he repeatedly failed the national test for vet certification."

With clowns like these driven solely by the profit motive in the breeding business, the magazine's sole wish is to see this silly Chihuahua boom, triggered by a loan-shark company's TV commercial, slink away with its tail between its legs. (MS)

KIDS FIND NEMOS, KILL THEM

Shukan Bunshun (January 22, 2004)

In "Finding Nemo," the animation blockbuster, a family of clownfish is decimated, first by undersea predators and then by man.

Man is in the form of a scuba diver, who captures Nemo, a cute young fish that ends up in the confines of an aquarium in a dentist's office.

The movie has been a smash hit in Japan since opening in December, raking in more than ¥8 billion in receipts. Many of its fans are moved by the story's emotionally delivered, pro-environmental message. *Shukan Bunshun*, however, finds this starkly ironic: The movie's massive popularity is having tragic consequences for Nemo's clownfish brethren living off Japan's shores.

The basic problem is that thousands of the movie's fans now want a Nemo of their own. That has pushed demand sky high at retailers for the exotic-looking fish, a trend which in turn is prompting divers and others to capture more and more of them—depleting their population drastically.

"Inquiries shot up from autumn [when the movie's PR campaign got under way], and when the movie opened in December our shipments jumped more than five-fold," says Hidetomo Kimura of HID Interaqtica, a Tokyo importer and seller of aquarium fish.

Clownfish have bright orange bodies with three broad vertical stripes and grow to around 10 cm (4 inches) in length. They sell for around ¥1,200 to ¥2,500 each. "They've always been popular because they're very cute, and for saltwater fish they're easy to raise," says Jun Ganaha of J's Aquarium in Okinawa Prefecture. Still, the sea waters not far from Ganaha's shop have been reeling under a very powerful "Nemo effect."

Local environmentalists tell the magazine they have spotted groups of people out at sea, who often destroy the coral, around which the fish live, and remove all the anemone—the undersea plants that serve as the fish's homes and egg-laying sites. "There have been cases in which every anemone and clownfish have been taken away from a site," one environmentalist complains.

Once the fish have been removed from their natural habitat, their chances of survival are a lot slimmer. That's because more and more clownfish owners are really more interested in Nemo the movie than caring for a saltwater fish.

"I bought my daughter a clownfish because she wanted a Nemo," a 31-year-old mother in Tokyo says. "I put it in a goldfish bowl filled with tap water and it died soon after." Other neophyte owners have been known to add table salt to tap water to replicate the sea water which the fish require to live.

A representative of Buena Vista International (Japan), which distributes "Finding Nemo," said the company regrets that some viewers have misunderstood the movie's message.

Yet even so, the company has struck a deal with Tetra Japan, a maker of home aquarium equipment, to use the movie to promote an aquarium set. What's more, the product is for raising freshwater—not saltwater—fish. The set features a picture of the famous Nemo—who would die if ever placed in such an aquarium. (GB)

BIG YEN FOR DEAD DOGGIES

Yomiuri Weekly (March 21, 2004)

"When Maiko came into our lives," Mami Takeda tells *Yomiuri Weekly*, "I felt as if I'd given birth to her."

The parent-child relationship deepened over the years. When, at age nine in 2002, Maiko died, Takeda and her husband, Hiromichi, were devastated. They took their tears to Tokyo District Court. How much is Maiko's life worth? ¥4.4 million, the plaintiffs insist.

The defendant is the family veterinarian. It was on his advice that Maiko was hospitalized, supposedly with diabetes, and under his care, apparently, that the white female Spitz died six months later. "Why didn't you give her insulin?" the Takedas demanded of the vet. There were other questions too. The vet's answers striking them as evasive, they sued.

Why ¥4.4 million? The Takedas' lawyer explains: "Suppose a human child is killed in a traffic accident. Damages would run to roughly ¥20 million. The human life expectancy is about 80 years. For a Spitz, it's 14. Fourteen-eightieths of ¥20 million is ¥3.5 million. Add medical costs, and you get a total of ¥4.4 million."

The logic is irrefutable, as long as you accept the premise: that human life and pet life are equivalent. More and more people, says *Yomiuri Weekly*, not only accept it, but, with Japan increasingly becoming a "pet society," take it for granted. And the courts, to the dismay of veterinarians, are backing them up.

Pet malpractice suits in Japan date back to 1986. The precedent-setting case involved a Tokyo vet who, operating on a dog, accidently left some gauze inside the animal. The dog died. The owners sued and won, their compensation award amounting to ¥50,000. That was consistent with the legal status of pets as property, as opposed to beings with a quasi-human right to life. So it went for the next decade or so, the awards so small they hardly seemed worth the trouble.

The turning point came in 1997. In January of that year, Osaka District Court heard a case concerning a pregnant cat that died after a dose of labor-inducing medication. The pregnancy meant more than one life was involved. The judge ordered the vet to pay a total of ¥800,000.

With that, the dam burst. In March 2002 a vet in Utsunomiya was ordered to pay ¥900,000 when the cat he was neutering died under the knife. Some eight months later, also in Utsunomiya, a man sued for ¥7.2 million when his 15-year-old pedigreed Shiba died during an operation. A suit filed in Tokyo District Court last August demands ¥5.3 million following the death from cancer of a beloved Labrador retriever.

In short, the Takedas are merely riding a wave. It is not the amount they are claiming, but a separate legal issue that sets their case apart. Their suit, *Yomiuri Weekly* explains, will be heard by a branch of the court specializing in medical malpractice suits involving human patients.

That, suggests a Tokyo University agriculture professor, may be carrying equivalency too far. (MH)

WILD BEAST ELUDES VILLAGERS

Shukan Taishu (September 20, 2004)

A 41-member search party trudges along the mountain trails that meander through the remote district of Shinsui, Hyogo Prefecture. The group members carry an odd collection of handmade nets and traps. Some poke through bushes, and others smoke out suspicious-looking holes in the ground. The group is on a dead-serious mission—to find a *tsuchinoko*, a mythical creature that has apparently been spotted many times throughout Japan over the years, but never caught.

On this day in late August, the "16th Mikata Tsuchinoko Expedition," an annual event, is combing an area where the beast was recently spotted. The report came on May 8 from 90-year-old Sugie Tanaka, a local farm woman.

"I was in the forest looking for bamboo shoots when I saw two round-shaped things. I thought they were two metallic-colored snakes, except I could see they had tails like rats," the woman recalls.

Many of the search-party members think the beast could only have been the tsuchinoko, Japan's version of Big Foot, although in this case the creature apparently has no feet. Rather, it's like a snake but with a much thicker body and a large round head, according to many of the accounts.

"My wife and I were out cutting grass in the morning and trying to kill any vipers, when she said, 'There's a huge snake!'" says Kazuaki Noda, 73, recalling an encounter in June 1994. "But its body was about as thick as a beer bottle and its head was like a tortoise's."

Noda reported the sighting to his local municipal office in Mikata, the town where the Shinsui district is located. His account was one of 58 received by Mikata, the highest number of tsuchinoko sightings anywhere in Japan. A large portion of the town's visitors, like the search-party members, come here solely for the purpose of spotting, and perhaps even snaring, the creature. "At this point, we don't talk about whether it exists or not, but, rather, how we are going to raise it once one has been caught," says Juichi Miyawaki, the search team's leader.

Yet, according to Naoki Yamaguchi, author of the book, *Catching the Illusionary Tsuchinoko*, efforts by groups like Miyawaki's are largely in vain. "The majority of the tsuchinoko encounters are by people who are laboring in the mountains or mountain-stream anglers or loggers. The number of sightings from people out on searches is barely one percent of the total," says Yamaguchi, who has interviewed more than 200 people claiming to have seen the creature.

Many scientists, meanwhile, don't appear impressed by this tsuchinoko phenomenon. After a villager living near Mikata submitted a purported tsuchinoko corpse in May to the Japan Snake Institute, based in Gunma Prefecture, its researchers determined the creature to be a rat snake. Similarly, when four loggers from another Hyogo Prefecture village arrived with suspicious reptilian remains in the spring of 2001, the institute deemed them to be from a common grass snake.

Still, such findings haven't dented the enthusiasm of Miyawaki and other tsuchinoko watchers, or even the town of Mikata. The municipality promises to give a large swath of the town's land to the first person who can produce a living tsuchinoko. (GB)

MEN DRESS IN LACY THINGS

Yomiuri Weekly (November 4, 2001)

"My bra and panties were stolen from the clothesline!" reads the outraged message on the electronic bulletin board.

"That's really sick," came one sympathetic reply.

"Unforgivable!" empathized another.

The above, incidentally, were all posted by men, who appear to be learning the hard way what it's like to be in a woman's shoes. Did we say shoes? Sorry. The stolen items were definitely not footwear. And as a general rule, says *Yomiuri Weekly*, the men who wear such items don't obtain them through theft.

These fellows, says the magazine, are neither gay nor cross dressers, but otherwise stalwart males who, for whatever reason, feel good when wearing bras under their business suits. What got them started? Talking shop at an *ofu-kai* (offline party), one says that as a teen, he mischievously slipped into his older sister's underwear to hide them from her. Another donned his first bra at the bidding of a lady friend and liked the feeling so much that he bought one for himself.

"When my wife was away caring for a parent, I ran out of clean undershorts and put on her panties instead," another relates. "Just for the hell of it, I tried on her bra. The sensation was unforgettable." One brief fitting and he was, er, hooked.

Then there's Koichi, a 50-ish section leader at a construction company. As his wife shopped for undergarments, she noticed an expression of longing on his face. "Do you want one too?" asked this *very* understanding woman. "Yes," he murmured.

Koichi theorizes that his interest in ladies' unmentionables stems from a desire to rebel against an unusually strict upbringing. Interestingly, the couple made no attempt to conceal his preference for feminine underthings from their two teenage daughters. Not that they really seem to mind. "Hey, if Dad likes it, then what's the big deal?" one asks.

Koichi's secret was almost exposed one rainy day, when he removed his wet jacket and a female co-worker saw, through his damp shirt, the telltale straps of a brassiere. "Let's keep it our little secret," she winked knowingly. But since then, Koichi has taken to wearing opaque undershirts over his bra. A guy can't be too careful, y'know.

Yomiuri Weekly introduces two Tokyo lingerie shops catering to both sexes. Vanilla Cube in Yotsuya, which opened last April, designates each Sunday "Men's Day." The shop also performs alterations to ensure a comfy fit. Okadaya Pearl Pink I, in Shinjuku, claims that roughly half its clientele are male. Middle-aged men can be seen browsing alongside female patrons, studiously sampling the tactile sensation of dainty lace underthings.

"A lot more men shop with us than I would have expected," says the lingerie floor manager at a major department store. Staff are instructed to treat them with customary deference—even when a customer tells them he's shopping for himself.

With gentlemen, as well as ladies, now determined to conceal secrets, lingerie maker Triumph's recently introduced metal-free bra, designed to pass through airport security devices without embarrassing the wearer, suddenly takes on an added appeal. (MS)

"HAGS" VANISH FROM TRENDY SPOTS

Spa! (April 1, 2001)

They kinda looked like pandas, with fluorescent make-up around their eyes and mouths. Their wild, dyed-blonde locks gave them the name *yamanba*, or mountain hags. And a couple of years ago, you could hardly go anywhere without seeing them staggering along in their micro-minis and platforms.

But now, *Spa!* says, the yamanba have pretty well disappeared, even from the streets of Tokyo's trendy Shibuya district—a place they once considered their own hallowed ground. "Girls around 20 were the first generation to really consider Shibuya their own. The only environments they'd really ever known were school and home. Then, for some unknown reason, from about '95 they just started hanging out around Shibuya. They made it their base to do as they liked," Chisako Wada, editor-in-chief of gotta-have teenzine *Popteen*, says.

"Once they'd found that base it probably gave birth to their street fashion. Up until then, any street fashion in Japan had been an imported one. Let's not forget the first street fashion in Japan was putting a hibiscus in your hair."

Wada continues, offering an explanation for the demise of the yamanba: "I suppose they were getting a little anxious. We had an enormous reaction to a recent special we ran on 'finding yourself.' It seems that wanting to find yourself so you feel strong is making these girls feel a bit ill at ease with their current lifestyles."

Perhaps the staff at 109, the Shibuya department store the yamanba made their Mecca, know more than anybody else about why the flamboyant femmes have suddenly gone mainstream.

"Now the girls who used to walk around with deeply tanned faces and the like have clearly adopted more adult-like tastes," a spokesman for the department store tells *Spa!* "It seems like we're welcoming the end of the culture that placed its prime focus on letting girls express their individuality in the most outrageous way."

Some of the former yamanba seem to agree. "I just got a little sick of all these people coming up to me and asking, 'What're you gonna do next? What're you gonna do next' I was always trying to think up some new trend," says Tomomi Kudo, once the pin-up girl of the mountain hag generation and now an aspiring celebrity. "It sort of got to the stage where I'd go outside and always be wondering what people were thinking about me."

Yoshika Tsukagawa, also a popular pin-up girl during the yamanba heyday but now an employee at a stall in 109, says that once so many other people got on to the black-faced bandwagon, she decided it was time to get off.

"Just as girls started to get deeper and deeper tans, I decided I'd do the same so I wouldn't miss out. The word yamanba didn't even exist then. But once people started calling us yamanba, things sort of changed," she says.

"It sort of became dirty. I'd done all that I could and could only follow others. I thought that if it had to be that way, I may as well act a bit more maturely. So I decided I no longer wanted to look like all the other girls." (RC)

YOUTHS SCAR OWN BODIES

Yomiuri Weekly (April 21, 2002)

Megumi, 24, is into scarification—puncturing her skin to make patterns of raised bumps, in her case on her belly. "It only takes 10 minutes with a knife to gouge your skin, but it's a lot of work to care for it afterward," she says. "You need to work at it to make the scars attractive."

This particular form of body decoration, explains *Yomiuri Weekly*, is common in Africa, because tattoos don't show up well on black skin. It is achieved by preventing the cuts from drying out, making them pustulate. (If the wounds heal promptly, they won't be as conspicuous.) To do this, one applies a mixture of butter, lemon and sugar—which is said to tingle like mad—until the process is completed in about 10 days.

Maria, 19, showed a rebellious streak from an early age. While still in her first year of middle school, she already had three apertures in each ear. Presently she sports five perforations on her genitals alone. And just below her collarbone is a tattoo of Hinotori (Space Firebird), the cartoon character made famous by the late cartoonist Osamu Tezuka, creator of Astro Boy.

Maria finds the limits of social tolerance odd. "Everybody tints their hair brown, but it's not okay to be blonde or some other color," she complains. "It's acceptable to pierce your ears, but not your nose. My parents say it's *my* body, so I'm the one responsible for what happens to it."

Once a month, aficionados of such extreme forms of adornment flock to Department H, a nightclub in Shibuya. The gathering resembles a casting session for a "Mad Max" sequel.

A cult favorite among the punctured crowd is "*Koroshiya 1* (Ichi The Killer)," a film about a nihilistic hero named Kakihara. The film, starring Tadanobu Asano, is chock-full of sadistic episodes designed to make audiences squirm and whimper. In one scene, Kakihara grasps a knife and slowly slices his own tongue. Just then his cell phone rings, and while he talks, blood streams from his mouth.

Koichi Negayama, professor of motivational studies at Waseda University, believes young people inflict pain on themselves as a means of affirming their identity. "In a world surrounded by virtual realities, they seek powerful sensations as a means of confirming they're alive," he says. "Young Japanese may feel that since society doesn't demand anything from them, the pain they inflict on their bodies is the only way of affirming themselves."

When *Yomiuri Weekly*'s reporter asked one young fellow what moved him to abuse his epidermis, he explained, "I'm interested in reconstructing my body." One form his reconstruction takes is a series of three metal rings embedded beneath the skin of his forearm. Another, as he demonstrates, was splitting the tip of his tongue, snake-like.

"I put a tourniquet around it before I cut it, so it hardly hurt at all," he hisses. (MS)

TEENS DROP BIKINIS, LAUNCH FAD

Shukan Gendai (September 6, 2003)

When 18-year-old Risa Kawabara and a young female friend headed out one day recently, they figured on spending a typical day at the beach. But after popping into a local video-game arcade, little did they know they would help launch one of this summer's biggest fads.

"We went there just wearing our swimsuits for some *purikura* (photos taken in a booth)," she recalls. "At first we did the usual poses but at one point we just said, 'Let's do it!'" In no time their bikinis came off. As the camera in the booth snapped away, the girls hammed it up in various sexy positions—and the fad was born.

It's called "*eropuri*," a Japanized contraction of "erotic" and "print," and it refers to teenage girls and young women having their photos taken in booths in the nude or nearly nude. Kawabara is a "queen of eropuri" and one of the fad's first exponents, according to *Shukan Gendai*.

The phenomena first came to the public's eye after *Popteen* magazine reported it in a special section of this year's September edition. "It's become a hit this summer mainly among girls from 15 to 20 years old," says Chisako Wada, *Popteen*'s chief editor. "It has basically spread by word of mouth among the girls." And it's spread like wildfire. Insert the term "eropuri" into the Yahoo Japan search engine and you'll get more than 300 hits.

In tracing the fad's evolution, *Shukan Gendai* points to developments in the technology of purikura machines along with the changing nature of game-arcade culture. The machines have advanced by leaps and bounds since their introduction in 1995. The wannabe models can now edit their pictures in all manner of ways and can have full-length body shots of themselves. In the past only unembellished portrait-style formats were available.

In the early years, teenage girls and young women, who make up the bulk of purikura customers, quickly became bored of simply smiling at the camera. So they began experimenting with their poses and facial expressions, with the result that their pics became sexier and sexier. The *"erokawaku"* (erotic-cute) had been a favorite purikura look until this summer, when the cute element gave way to outright eroticism.

Also behind the eropuri boom is a trend to take pics while dressed in elaborate costumes, known as *"kosupurei"* (costume play). Many video arcades have catered to this by installing changing rooms. Thus girls and women no longer feel self-conscious when taking their clothes off at the arcades, *Shukan Gendai* explains.

Kawabara has posed nude not only with her female friends but also with her boyfriend. She says she gives the racy photo-decals to her boyfriend or other female friends. She cringes at the thought of selling them as pornography. Other girls say they give their racy pics to guys they want to impress.

"Girls are filled with aspirations and yearnings," says Ira Ishida, an author who focuses on youth issues. "Purikura allows them to enjoy themselves by feeling like they're sexy models, in the same way that karaoke makes people feel like they're famous singers." (GB)

BUSTS EXPAND
AS ECONOMY SHRINKS

dacapo (October 15, 2003)

dacapo convenes an all-girl symposium to talk about . . . breasts. Is it true they're getting bigger? It is. The statistics are clear. Japanese bosoms have swelled, on average, 2.5 cm over the past 20 years.

"It's heredity," says Kaori Kawai, 90-cm, E-cup. "My mom's F-cup."

"Really? I don't know," demurs Harumi Nemoto, a 103-cm, I-cup girl. "My mom had small breasts . . ."

"As for me," confides Yuka Igarashi, an 86-cm D-cup, "I used to pray, 'Grow, breasts, grow.' And strangely enough, little by little, they did! Some girls have complexes about their large breasts," Yuka muses thoughtfully. "Others use them as weapons. Men are so simpleminded. It's so easy to get a rise out of them."

That it is. But let's penetrate a bit deeper. What's behind this shapely revolution?

Physiology, for one thing. Menstruation, *dacapo* learns, begins on average two years earlier today than it did 20 years ago, giving the body an additional two years to blossom under the influence of estrogen. Why are girls menstruating earlier? "Because," suggests one authority, "elementary schools serve more nutritious lunches than they used to."

That's one theory. There are others—among them, that the proliferation of erotic magazines, movies, videos and so on stimulates the production of female hormones.

Sex itself might stimulate it. Are girls sexually active earlier because their bodies mature earlier, or is it the other way around? Either way, early sexual activity among girls is an established fact. Research by the Japan Sex Education Council shows 24 percent of high-school girls acknowledged being sexually active in 1999, up from 14 percent in 1993 and nine percent in 1987.

Boys, meanwhile, are maturing later than they used to, partly, it seems, as a result of so-called "hormone receptors," pollutants that mimic female hormones. Come to think of it, says *dacapo*, these could be yet another factor behind girls' early maturation.

In the reading room at the Education Ministry, the magazine stumbled upon some dusty old files of unusual interest. The papers show the progression of bust size, prefecture by prefecture, among third-year high-school girls over a span of four-and-a-half decades, from 1950 to 1994. (In 1995 the ministry deleted bust measurement from forms recording students' height, weight and other indicators—a matter of "privacy," it explained.)

In 1950, the documents show, the national average bust size among the students was 79.8 cm. In 1994 it was 82.6 cm. In 1950, Japan's most buxom prefecture was Kyoto, but immediately thereafter the honor shifted to the Tohoku region, whose six prefectures have shared it among themselves ever since.

Does any of this matter? Why, yes. The size and prominence of the human mammary glands have no animal equivalent, *dacapo* hears from a biologist. Large breasts, he says, are an evolutionary contrivance designed to keep roving men home caring for their families. Interesting, the article adds (somewhat fancifully), that the swelling Japanese bosom should correspond so closely to the economic downturn. Is heightened economic competition spurring evolutionary change? The "!?" with which the magazine concludes suggests it rather hopes so. (MH)

SCHOLARS FIND WORLD IS COMIC

Sunday Mainichi (May 23, 2004)

Doraemon, as the world knows, is a 22nd-century cat-robot, or robot-cat, possessed of some remarkable attributes, such as a fear of mice and an abdomen full of marvelous "tools," among them a flight-enabling propeller and a time machine.

Time magazine dubbed him Japan's cutest export. Star of *manga*, TV and movies, he has been delighting children of all ages since 1969, and now, reports *Sunday Mainichi*, when the children grow up they can study him at university.

Doraemonology? Toyama University does indeed offer this elective. Its official title is "Doraemon's World," and Yoshiyuki Yokoyama has been teaching the noncredit course for six years. He has a ready answer to bemoaners of the academic decline supposedly symbolized by such fare. "It is prejudice," he says, "to view manga as low-brow. That's outdated thinking." Manga, he believes, "are the best thing contemporary Japanese literature has going for it."

It's not only one course at one university. At Kanazawa Industrial College, the featured techno-hero is Gundam, the anime robot warrior. Students are not analyzing his adventures, but his construction—they are future engineers, after all.

"We conceived of the course"—which like Doraemon's World is noncredit—"as something to stimulate students' interest in making things," says Taro Matsuo, who was instrumental in putting the program together. "These days you get a lot of students saying, 'What should I make? I can't think of anything to do.' If they can get ideas from anime, why not?"

Kyoto Seika University, in 2000, introduced manga studies into its fine arts faculty—partly for the drawing techniques to be learned, but also, explains Professor Keiichi Makino, "to get students thinking about the origins and history of manga culture, because we want our students to have a global grasp of manga production."

And then there's the venerable University of Tokyo. Beginning this fall, says *Sunday Mainichi*, this ultrastaid, hypercerebral molder of past, present and presumably future elite bureaucrats will offer a program for budding creators of anime and computer games. The world has changed, and this is as good a measure of it as any.

Any student who thinks Doraemonology is a matter of sitting back and watching Doraemon reruns is soon disillusioned. At the aforementioned Toyama University, data analysis is Professor Yokoyama's emphasis. How many scenes focus on the main character? With what degree of frequency does he make use of his secret tools? What does all this *mean*? It's pretty sober stuff, and the high dropout rate attests to disappointed expectations of a leisurely romp through cartoon-land.

Perhaps it would never have happened had the student-age population not dipped. "All universities are struggling desperately to attract students," notes social critic Kiyoshi Shimano. "And so they jump on the bandwagon of whatever is fashionable at the moment. That's true especially of the lesser-known universities. Manga courses and the like are great PR for them."

There's a good deal more to it than that, counters Kyushu University researcher Midori Hinoshita. "Manga and anime," she says, "are unique products of Japanese culture. Considering their economic scale and social influence, they merit in-depth research."

Shimano stands his ground. Mangaology, he argues, "may give professors an opportunity to do appealing research, but what kind of future does it give students?" (MH)

COSTUMED LOVERS SEEK SEX THRILLS

Spa! (August 24, 2004)

Once upon a time, *cosupure H* was only for *otaku,* nerds whose exclusive cultivation of one hobby or fetish gives them their characteristic withdrawn air. But lately, *Spa!* finds, it's trickling down to the masses. Now you too can clothe Eros in his true colors.

"Cosupure" is a katakana neologism for costume play. "H" means sex. Costume-play sex. Or, to borrow *Spa!*'s English, "costume Eros." Nagisa, 19, is a believer. "I like role playing," she says. "Like, I'm in my bathing suit, it's swimming class, and my boyfriend's the teacher. I even write lines for us. He's embarrassed and has a hard time getting into the role, but I think he'll come around."

"What's the point?" grumbles her prosaic boyfriend. "We just get naked anyway." Usually, the magazine points out, it's the guy who pushes costume play, but Nagisa is the prime mover in her relationship. Having learned of it from partners encountered in the casual sex-for-cash transactions known as *enjo-kosai,* she has taken on the mission of refining her boyfriend's sexual tastes.

Costume-play love hotels are springing up to meet a growing demand—as are costume-play image clubs (an "image club" or *imekura* is a sex-play venue, the staff being the playmates) and costume-play bars. They sport names like Casanova and Saint Cosplay Academy. At one costume-play love hotel *Spa!* finds 20-odd costumes available—maid, policewoman, nurse, waitress and so on. The Saint Cosplay Academy image club boasts over 200.

So, gentlemen, what's your fancy? Nun? OL? Stewardess? Manga or *anime* character? High-school girl? Easy. Your wish is no sooner spoken than granted, with no outrage to morality or decency. In cosupure H, clothes make the woman, the woman makes the man, and you, sir—why, you have it made.

The magazine notes a distinction between otaku and non-otaku costume players: For the latter, cosupure is an erotic stimulus pure and simple, while the former relish it for its own sake—not that "H" may not follow. Non-otaku tend to prefer "realistic" costumes, the better to fuel their erotic fantasies; otaku favor fantastic garb in the hope of expanding reality.

"Humans," observes a plastic surgeon to *Spa!* "are beings who seek beauty in prototypes." With due respect to his professional expertise, it is tempting to argue that, on the contrary, humans are beings who seek beauty in the individual. On the other hand, cosupure H seems to bear him out.

"One day," recalls Emi, 21, "my boyfriend said to me, 'Let me see you in your high-school uniform.' So I put on my old sailor suit for him"—and discovered the joy, the marvelous erotic rush, of symbolically returning to childhood as a sexually charged adult.

She and he became dedicated cosu-players. When they broke up, she took possession of their entire costume wardrobe—except for the maid suit. "Let me have that," said the boyfriend, "for my next girlfriend." Graciously, Emi agreed. (MH)

Soft on Demand, Japan's prime purveyor of puerile pornography, is celebrating the release of the 50th of its "All Nude" series which has seen uncovered young women cover almost the entire spectrum of Japanese society, reports *Flash*.

SOD started the All Nude series with the release in April 1996 of "All Nude Audition," a movie featuring dozens of young women performing on the casting couch.

Ganari Takahashi, SOD's president and the originator of the All Nude series, used the know-how he picked up while working in television to produce saucy movies similar to variety shows screened on the smaller screen and ensured all the performers were women working stark naked.

"Other companies copied us, which sort of felt like they were praising us, and that made me feel wonderful. When [legendary porn auteur] Toru Nishimura made the Completely Nude All Nude Awards show, it was awesome," Takahashi says. "It was just sensational that the ace of the adult video world would make a movie about me, a new kid on the block."

Among the classics in the All Nude series has been January's *All Nude Ballet*, where a group of veteran prima donnas cast aside their pride and danced "Swan Lake" in the raw before 100 people to make enough money to finance a trip overseas.

Maintaining the highly cultured air of the series was the *All Nude Orchestra*, which was released in September 2002. The movie was actually filmed documentary style, with all those who appeared in the buff also polished performers and the girls unwilling to pull their weight summarily expelled from the music group.

Those appearing in the *All Nude Wadaiko* edition of July this year played to a beat of a different drum—literally. The sirens on stage stripped down to their birthday suits while beating out a mighty tune on traditional Japanese drums known as wadaiko.

So was *All Nude Moving*, the April 1998 release in which naked ladies performed the job of removalists. SOD had just secured new, larger offices to coincide with its development as Japan's fastest growing video maker. Taking advantage of the situation, and displaying some of the nouse that sparked its phenomenal growth, SOD got the girls to do the heavy work while in the buff and made a hit movie out of it at the same time.

Even SOD's disaster movies have been a roaring success when they've been part of the All Nude bunch. *All Nude Evacuation Drill* came out in November 1996 while the Great Hanshin Earthquake of the previous January was still fresh in peoples' mind and marked Japan's renewed vigor in approaching evacuation procedures in the wake of a natural disaster, proving that drills can even be performed without clothes.

Naturally, with so many women putting on a show while showing everything, it'd be fairly cold nearly any time of the year. But few of the All Nude series works can approach the one released in April 1997, where a bevy of buff beauties re-enacted a legendary hike a late 19th-century Japanese army troop made through sleet and snow. *All Nude Snow-Capped Mountain Hiking* proved to be the coolest of the 50 works as the 10 performers bravely strode through the snow in freezing conditions, ignoring any threat to life or limb and the obvious fear they felt.

"Ahhh," the magazine quotes performer Kei Hiramatsu screaming during *All Nude Snow-Capped Mountain Hiking*. "I don't want to die while I'm completely nude." (RC)

LONELY LUNCH-GOERS LOSE IT

Yomiuri Weekly (April 8, 2001)

It was around last autumn that Akiko had her nervous break-down. The 22-year-old had been suffering from insomnia and depression, and for several days she couldn't bring herself to go to her job at a mid-size trading company in Tokyo.

After she checked into a mental health clinic, doctors pinpointed the cause of her suffering—her lunch hours. Ever since her university days, Akiko had eaten the mid-day meal with a group of her closest friends. But her boss had made her end the practice, obliging her to dine with her company colleagues instead. Her fear of losing her friends forever proved to be an unbearable psychological strain, and she cracked.

Akiko is among a rapidly growing number of young Japanese who suffer from "lunch-mate syndrome," *Yomiuri Weekly* says. For them, the lunch hour is critical to their psychological well-being. They use the chance to bond, either with friends or workplace colleagues, and when deprived of that opportunity, they can easily suffer a plight similar to Akiko's.

Shizuo Machizawa, a psychiatrist at Rikkyo University, tells the magazine that lunch-mate syndrome emerged about seven years ago. Sufferers tend to be the type who have a strong sense of affiliation to others and fear being alone. When not accompanied by close acquaintances at lunchtime, many simply lose their appetites. Another symptom is a sense of isolation, stemming from the belief that eating alone is somehow a humiliating experience.

The result is often depression and an intense fear of going to work. Most of the victims are women, although the number of male sufferers is growing particularly quickly. Machizawa says the condition becomes especially prevalent in spring, when the entry-level recruits start their new jobs.

"At this time, it's critically important to be approached to be someone's lunch mate. That's particularly true in the case of women. As they form extremely tightly knit groups among themselves, it's difficult to join once the groups have been set up," he says.

Yomiuri Weekly suggests the condition is a sign of the times. For many members of the younger generation, it says, social lunches are a definite lifestyle priority, ranking higher in importance than even their jobs or the demands of their bosses. (GB)

THEY SAID IT IN THE *Weeklies*

"There's nothing I hate more than having to stand beside my boss at the urinals in the company washroom. So I go into a stall and sit in privacy."

—23-year-old company employee, one of a growing number of males who prefer to urinate while in a seated position, to *Shukan Bunshun* (December 18, 2003)

EMPLOYEES BOXED BY BOSSES

Yomiuri Weekly (May 19, 2002)

Welcome to the corporate "restructure box." It comes in various shapes and sizes. It can be a corridor, a locker room, a dark corner of a warehouse for you and your desk. For Shinichi Yamamura, it was each in turn. The restructure box is not meant to restructure you, exactly. It's meant to eject you—and thus restructure the company.

But Yamamura, 38, didn't cooperate. He refused to quit. For months he endured the corporate equivalent of solitary confinement. In the end, he won, and finally got posted to a real job. Now that the grand prize is his, however, he's no longer sure he wants it. The ordeal, says *Yomiuri Weekly*, left him with grave doubts about "what's important in life."

Restructure boxes are cropping up in many companies. The spaces' most obvious common features are negatives—no phones, no computers, no windows, no work. You more or less just sit there, wondering what you did to deserve this descent into absurdity.

You may have done nothing. No matter. There are agencies that specialize in making the innocent *look* guilty, the competent *seem* useless. They're called *yamesaseya*—professionals whose expertise is "making people quit"—and to them, no one is blameless. If an employee hasn't stolen money, he's probably filched copy paper. If he doesn't goof off, he surely catnaps in the company car from time to time. Or perhaps he buys a discount air ticket, claims for full fare and pockets the difference.

Tail him long enough and they'll catch him in the act of *something.* Present him with the incriminating photographs and hope he goes quietly. If not—into the restructure box with him. The yamesaseya's fee isn't cheap; nor, of course, is the salary the boxed employee continues to draw until he succumbs to frustration or depression and leaves. But the firm saves severance pay and thus comes out ahead.

In a contracting economy, there are all kinds of reasons to shed aging loyal employees. They haven't kept up with the times; a bloated payroll is a drain on shrinking profits; bright energetic young graduates sit idle, awaiting vacancies.

But Yamamura's case was different. Having been hired from another company, he never quite fitted in with colleagues who'd been recruited straight out of university. When he began blowing the whistle on what struck him as shoddy management, his fate was sealed. "Yamamura," said his boss, indicating a corridor, "here's your new workplace."

Months later, he was relocated to a locker room. Colleagues trooping through in the morning gaped at him. Then they turned away in embarrassment. What was there to say? They knew it could have as easily been them, and that one day it might be.

His next restructure box was a warehouse. "Clean up the place," he was told. It was a job, at least. "For Japanese salarymen," an expert tells the *Yomiuri Weekly*, "the worst thing is not to be put to work. They develop all kinds of psychosomatic illnesses."

Yamamura appealed to the Labor Standards Bureau—in vain. Alone, with no outside support, his only weapon was his seemingly inexhaustible patience and some good advice. "The company can't pay you to do nothing forever," said an acquaintance who had been through a similar mill. "It will have to come to an end sooner or later."

In the warehouse, Yamamura developed a fondness for an old portable heater he unearthed from some dusty corner. It actually worked, easing the damp chill of the otherwise unheated room. His last words in the warehouse before the company capitulated and returned him to the corporate ladder were addressed to the heater: "I won't let them throw you away. I'll take you home with me." (MH)

WORKING HARD AT GOOFING OFF

Sunday Mainichi (December 8, 2002)

"There's nothing like a soak in a hot bath to get you out of a slump," Masataka Yamamoto, an authority on hot springs, advises the *Sunday Mainichi*.

Yamamoto, formerly the president of Oki Data Corporation, favors the Hotel Hanshin, a mineral spring in Osaka's Fukushima Ward that charges visitors ¥2,500 to come in for a good relaxing soak.

The magazine has advice for Tokyoites as well, introducing similar facilities at Tokyo Kua, located adjacent to the entrance to JR Tokyo Station (admission ¥2,300), or the Junisha Onsen, a natural hot spring (Tokyo, amazingly, has well over a dozen bubbling beneath its concrete surface) at Nishi-Shinjuku 4-chome (¥1,900).

What exactly are these pages? Yet another vacation advisory?

Not quite. *Sunday Mainichi*'s listing of bathhouses, libraries, aquariums and theaters is intended to shed light on one of Japan's best-kept secrets: Its loyal worker bees not only seek amusement after a hard day's work, but also engage in goofing off creatively while on the job.

Indeed, the practice is so widespread that the verb *saboru*—derived from the English "sabotage"—was coined years ago to mean goofing off on company time. "The more seriously a person performs his work, the more he needs to goof off a little," asserts Nagahiro Uno, a director at the Fuji Research Institute.

The practice of saboru appears to be widespread in Japan. When the magazine surveyed 50 salaried workers in front of Tokyo's

Shinbashi Station, only 32 percent denied ever having goofed off. Of those who admitted to the practice, the most common activity was hanging out in a coffee shop (36 percent), followed by ambling around a nearby park (8 percent). Playing pachinko or arcade games and loafing in the car were both cited by 4 percent.

Other methods of slipping away for a little rest and relaxation included sitting in a hotel lobby, exercising at a gym, visiting a bookstore and playing the stock market. "Essentially, as long as people work in a company, they can't detach themselves from their main function, which is performing work," says Asato Izumi, a former salaryman-turned-author.

"That's all the more reason why they need some 'personal time' to themselves. Going out to lunch with coworkers doesn't give them the chance to change their mood—it needs to be something that's personally enjoyable."

Sabotage, says the magazine, comes in three basic categories: *iyashi* (emotional healing), seeking knowledge and laughter.

And, in a move not likely to endear itself to the corporate world, it provides a clip-and-save listing of 20 places it recommends that are proximate to the main business districts of Tokyo and Osaka. Among them are the Suzumoto theater in Ueno and Suehirotei at Shinjuku, which both host daylong *rakugo* (comic monologue) performances and other traditional forms of stage entertainment.

"The more a person becomes occupied with his work, the bigger a mental block can occur," says Fuji Research Institute's Uno. "Under such circumstances, goofing off that enhances decisiveness or lifts one's mood should be regarded as a productive use of work time." (MS)

OFFICE DEPRESSION CREATES ADDICTS

Yomiuri Weekly (July 4, 2004)

On a recent morning, 26-year-old Masami woke up in her apartment to discover a stack of 10 uneaten *bento* boxes. "Did I buy all those?" she asked herself. But when she tried to remember the events of the preceding night, her mind drew a complete blank.

The experience has become frighteningly common for Masami, a TV news reporter. On another morning, for instance, she discovered that her trousers were soaked and her shoes caked in mud, for some unknown reason, although she suspected that the culvert running near her home was somehow involved.

According to the *Yomiuri Weekly*, Masami's memory-loss problem stems from an addiction to sleeping pills. She began taking the medication after suffering bouts of insomnia, brought on by the demands of her high-pressure job. At first, the pills helped but then she gradually supplemented her prescription with over-the-counter products, tripling the original dosage. Her inability to remember things that happened just hours earlier has become a side effect of that drug dependency.

Addictions like Masami's appear to be spreading rapidly in Japan. Those who are at particular risk are people like her: young, ambitious white-collar types, who, by all exterior appearances, seem to be successful and brimming with confidence.

"More and more people are depressed these days, while addictive behavior stemming from feelings of melancholy is also growing," says psychologist Chikako Ogura, who blames the problem on an increasingly jittery and ruthless work environment.

"Japanese companies are grappling with structural problems. It's an era in which even large companies go bankrupt. Even within the company, workers fear being laid off due to restructuring, while competition is getting tougher due to the adoption of performance-based systems of promotions," she says.

One remarkable aspect of this phenomenon is the wide range of addictions to which people are succumbing. In addition to the common addictions like drugs and alcohol are such activities as compulsive shopping, using phone chat-lines, patronizing fortune-tellers and surfing the Internet.

For Akira, a 36-year-old car salesman, the addiction is women. Thanks to a flexible work schedule, he has managed to cultivate several "sex friends," with whom he indulges in frequent sexual interludes during the day. The affairs are fun while they last, Akira admits. But lately the aftereffect has turned into chronic feelings of remorse, which in his worst moments shift into self-disgust. The feelings have become so dark and frequent that he has sought counseling.

Naohisa Nakamura, an associate professor at Kurume University, says it's common for depressed and stressed-out men to become addicted to the pursuit of women. "In many of the cases, the partners are older," he says. "It's easy for men with immature personalities to develop addictions for women, since their bonds with their mothers are excessively strong," he says.

So are you suffering from a work-related dependency, or prone to one? Just ask yourself the following twelve questions, compiled by *Yomiuri Weekly*:

- ☑ Are your conversations limited to work?
- ☑ Do you spend all day worrying about small mistakes?
- ☑ Do you forgo dating opportunities to work overtime instead?
- ☑ Do you occasionally bring your work home with you?

☑ Have you refrained from using your paid holiday time?

☑ Do you think about your work even during holidays?

☑ Do you get angry when friends keep you waiting?

☑ Do you pick up the phone the split second it rings?

☑ Are you constantly hounded by deadlines?

☑ Do you become uneasy when your underlings or co-workers are given assignments at work?

☑ Do you refrain from socializing with people who aren't particularly job-oriented?

☑ Do you believe your co-workers to be incompetent?

If six or more of your answers were "yes," then beware. If the number is at least nine, then there's a good chance you have already developed a dependency. (GB)

THEY SAID IT IN THE *Weeklies*

"I've seen one puppy with severely crossed legs, another missing its lower jaw and a third that ate like a horse but vomited everything up half an hour later. None of them lived long."

—Veterinarian to *Asahi Geino* about the growing practice of inbreeding among some breeders (June 5, 2003)

Weekly Playboy (September 14, 2004)

Before the summer heat subsides, *Weekly Playboy* gets in one last round of spine-chilling tales, as Japanese are wont to do to find relief from the sweltering weather. But instead of haunted houses or cemeteries, the magazine serves up a selection of stories set in modern-day office buildings. Are they based on actual events? We can't say for certain. But several jilted OLs (or "office ladies," as Japanese refer to female white-collar workers) fully demonstrate the truth to the old adage "Hell hath no fury like a woman scorned."

"I'd been going with this guy in the office for three years and we were all set to get married," relates 26-year-old Fumiko, who works at a communications firm. "Then he meets some biddy at a party and drops me for her. I found out later he even told the girl about me, saying, 'She's like my mother—I can't make love to her.'

"But I couldn't give him up. So I told him I was pregnant. I even borrowed ultrasound scans from a friend who's four months along, to show him. 'Look how big our baby is already,' I'd say and smile, watching his horrified expression. And I'd keep feeding him little reminders, like, 'Today I go for a doctor's examination,' or 'We'll be parents before much longer.'

"You could see he was losing weight, and he made a serious mistake in his work. I began feeling sorry for him and told him I'd decided to have an abortion. He began weeping and blubbered gratitude to me for letting him off the hook."

Another goosebump-raising tale is that of Kikue, 26, who quit her job when she saw her office paramour with his family. But that wasn't the end of the story.

"I took a part-time job in the convenience store on the first floor of the condo in which he lived. One day, he strolled in and I cheerfully greeted him. He took one look at me and froze in his tracks.

"After that, he never came back to the store; but I got to be quite friendly with his wife and 3-year-old daughter. It even got to the point that the wife was telling me how much their daughter liked me.

"About the second month I was on the job, his wife invited me up to their apartment and began pouring her heart out to me about how she couldn't stand his mother. She was so happy to be able to share her innermost feelings. Anyway, just before I left, I went to the washbasin and propped up a semi-nude photo I'd shot of him in bed.

"The next day, I quit my job. I don't know what happened with him and his wife after that."

Weekly Playboy's onomatopoetic reaction to this act of feminine guile (and we translate here literally) was "*Joooooo*" (the sound of incontinence).

"The less experienced a woman, the more fearsome her response to being scorned. It's something men had better not forget," the magazine is advised by Chocho-san, the nom de plume of an authoress who worked both as a Ginza nightclub hostess and in an office.

Indeed, sighs the weekly to its young male readers, those office ladies can be truly terrifying creatures. And in spite of such fearsome consequences as the examples above, you say you *still* want to take them out and show them a good time? (MS)

MURPHY'S LAW— JAPAN-STYLE

Yomiuri Weekly (September 9, 2001)

The oft-quoted Murphy's Law is attributed to Edward A. Murphy, Jr., an American engineer who conducted rocket-sled experiments for the U.S. Air Force. The law states: "If anything can go wrong, it will."

Yomiuri Weekly provides original insights into why things always go wrong—with an authentic Japanese twist. Some examples:

Law of Inauspicious Timing   If you stay home nearly all morning, but nip out for the briefest of errands, you'll find a nondelivery notification slip from the post office or a parcel-delivery service.

The Kuroneko Adjunct   On the day you absolutely don't leave the house, there is no possibility that a registered letter or parcel will arrive.

The Obverse Conundrum   People collecting payment for newspaper delivery or NHK will always show up when you are at home.

Days of the Weak   The morning you oversleep is invariably on a collection day for combustible rubbish, which means you're then stuck with it.

The Little Lost Cabby   Whenever you find yourself in an unfamiliar place, the driver of the cab you flag down won't know the place either.

Give the Meter Its Due   The fare on the meter always jumps to the next figure the moment you tell the driver to halt.

Fickle Weather Factors   Wash and wax your car and then water your flowers on a gorgeous day . . . that then turns showery. Similarly, if you leave home without an umbrella, it will rain.

Negative Splash Flow   The umbrella you lose is always an expensive brand-name model. Flimsy plastic ones last forever.

Tormented Soles   On the day you wear those expensive new shoes, nothing less than a major flood will occur.

Bathroom Trauma   It's always you who gets the last square of paper and has to replace the roll. Likewise when the shampoo runs out.

Laws of the Laundry   It always starts raining on days when you run a huge load, including a blanket, and you've got no space to hang it anywhere indoors.

Unhappy Ending   You always find the most interesting program on TV when it's precisely five minutes from the conclusion.

Please Pass the V-Chips   Whenever the whole family's in a mellow mood and gathered together in front of the telly, the program being shown will inevitably feature an embarrassing sex scene.

Well, there you have it, says *Yomiuri Weekly*. Think ahead and plan meticulously, but remember, there's no escaping the inevitability that things are sure to go wrong. (MS)

AUTOMAKER'S AD INSULTS JAPANESE

Shukan Shincho (December 13, 2001)

Japanese have often been criticized overseas for taking a racist attitude toward others. Pleas of innocence resulting from ignorance are often derided and the reputation of Japanese suffers further damage.

But the recent actions of automaker Daihatsu Motor Co. suggest the Japanese really may not have had a clue about touchy racial issues after all, if *Shukan Shincho* is anything to go by.

A commercial for Daihatsu's extremely successful Max compact car began airing on Japanese TV in the first week of November. It featured a Japanese woman driving the car through the streets of a typical European town. Each person the woman drove past—from an elderly couple to a young woman to a policeman—greeted her by placing their index fingers on the edge of their eyes and pulling them back to show her a "slant-eyes" face.

"When I first saw it, I couldn't believe it," says a trading company employee with many years of living in Europe under his belt. "Everybody who appears in the commercial was giving her a 'slant-eyes' face. It's an expression whites use to poke fun at Orientals."

He continues, "In Austria, for instance, making that face and saying, 'Chink, Chank, Chon' is used to taunt Orientals. Any Japanese who's lived in the West for some length of time has had the unfortunate experience of being subjected to this insult at least once."

Following several complaints about the commercial, Daihatsu was forced to drag it from the airwaves. From the second week of November, TV viewers have been greeted by a similar commercial featuring the same people but without the "slant-eyes" gestures made in the earlier version. Daihatsu officials are apologetic.

"We only ever wanted to use the gestures to emphasis the sleek design of the headlights on the Max," a company spokesman says. "Nobody picked up on this in pre-screening tests we did with viewers. However, we are terribly sorry to have upset some viewers in a manner we never dreamed of."

Some are critical of the lax attitude the Japanese take toward racial issues. "I don't know whether it's because we grow up on this isolated island, but Japanese are just naive when it comes to problems like this," a media commentator gripes to *Shukan Shincho*. "Thank god it was Japanese insulting Japanese. If it had been Jews or even Muslims that were insulted there would have been an uproar." (RC)

THEY SAID IT IN THE *Weeklies*

"This is not something amateurs should be trying at home. I can only do it because I go to the gym six times a week and have an incredibly flexible member that is way longer than that of the average Japanese."

—Porn star Miki Yanai to *Weekly Playboy*, regarding the "Helicopter" sex technique which earned him an invitation to a party at Yale University (December 14, 2004)

CELL PHONE RAGE TURNS VIOLENT

Shukan Taishu (May 6, 2002)

The scene is from a TV commercial for Sapporo beer, and its hero is someone many of us can empathize with.

We see Koichi Hamada, a crusty political commentator, blabbering away in a loud voice into his cell phone while on a train. An irritated fellow passenger, a middle-aged man, can't take it any longer. He gets out of his seat, grabs the annoying Hamada by the scruff of his leathery neck and tosses him out of the train.

In fact, this is not an uncommon scene these days in Japan. As cell phones have proliferated, the number of arguments, scuffles and even violent confrontations sparked by their use has skyrocketed.

The problem is that many of their users lack discretion, etiquette or common sense when chattering away or sending e-mail, says *Shukan Taishu*. The magazine comes to that conclusion after listening to the experiences of a number of victims and witnesses of inconsiderate cell phone users. One such witness is an unnamed salaryman in his 30s, who recounts the time he spotted a mother on a bicycle.

"She was on a bike with her daughter, who must have been in the first or second grade of elementary school and was sitting in the back seat. The mother was pedaling her bike while holding her cell phone in one hand and tapping out e-mail on it. "As you'd expect, she lost balance, hit a telephone pole and tumbled the bike over. The girl, who was flung from her seat, started crying."

But that wasn't the most chilling part of the story, the magazine says. The mother simply put the girl, now with a bleeding elbow, back in the seat and rode off—continuing with her e-mail.

The magazine's other stories include youths who chose toilet cubicles in public washrooms or train seats for the elderly to make their phone calls or write their e-mail. One man reports an oblivious pedestrian, chatting away on his phone and colliding into him. The pedestrian apologized—but only to the caller on the other end of the line for letting the collision cause an interruption in their conversation.

Then there's the man who had to explain to police in Saitama Prefecture earlier this month why he punched out a train passenger next to him. He simply got tired of being constantly poked by the passenger's arm and elbow as the passenger furiously typed an e-mail.

"Public spaces are areas where at least a minimal level of manners and propriety should be observed," says social commentator Ryoko Ozawa. "More and more people, however, are seeing these as their private areas. That's why the amount of friction and the number of attacks are increasing."

Japan is now a nation obsessed with cell phones. There are more than 80 million of the devices, surpassing the 50 million odd landline phones.

"Japan is in a kind of eerie situation right now," Ozawa says. "People are doing their e-mail all the time and any time, and everywhere, be it in trains or restaurants. But I wonder if they really have all that much business to take care of." (GB)

JUDGES TAKE TURN IN DOCK

Shukan Gendai (June 15, 2002)

Judges in Japan were once viewed with the same sense of awe reserved for, as the saying goes, "saints or princes." Maybe this is why their personality quirks have seldom drawn much public attention.

How things have changed, reports *Shukan Gendai*. One possible cause for this observation occurred last year when Yasuhiro Muraki, a Tokyo High Court judge, was found guilty on multiple counts of abetting teen prostitution.

The timing couldn't have been better for a book, and as it happened, "Who's Who of Judges," a work chock-full of information and insights on 115 Tokyo judges, made its appearance last month. Not surprisingly, it's been selling like proverbial hot cakes.

According to the book, at the disgraced Judge Muraki's trial, presiding Judge Megumu Yamamuro minced few words, blasting his colleague as "[a man with] a Lolita complex, an old lecher . . ."

Yamamuro also once ordered two young defendants charged in the fatal beating of a fellow rail commuter to reflect on the error of their ways by listening to peace songs crooned by Masashi Sada, a folk singer.

"The book was planned from last year, and we tapped the skills of an extensive range of people involved in the law, especially attorneys," says the book's publisher. "I read it and thought, 'Wow,'" raves Shoji Takamizawa, a noted attorney. "These aren't just superficial profiles, they really get down to the nitty-gritty. I don't know how the writers obtained all the details, but I suppose there's going to be a hunt to find who leaked this stuff."

Hirokichi Koike, another judge featured in the book, not only has a reputation for unpredictability but is fond of quoting from such ancient sages as Dogen (a 13th-century Zen priest) when delivering his verdicts. "Koike even did this once when sentencing a foreigner, and the poor court interpreter had a terrible time of it," a lawyer recalls.

"Along with the eccentric judges, some are downright incompetent," remarks Kazuo Washimi, a legal journalist. "Take Minoru Okamura of the Hachioji District Court, who caused a procedural mistrial by accidentally deleting a key passage when he typed out his ruling on a word processor."

But, asks the magazine, why are judges like Muraki, who stoop to criminal activities, apparently on the increase?

"Well, due to their heavy workload, they're probably under a lot of stress," suggests Washimi. "They most likely spent their younger years totally immersed in study. In such an insulated, sterile environment, they're totally out of it."

While the book delivers some harsh verdicts, *Shukan Gendai* nevertheless notes that "Who's Who" lauds a few others. Like Takashi Sonoge, who, while at the University of Tokyo, belonged to a group that studied *rakugo* (comic storytelling). When he gave his ruling on a recent libel suit, he tacked on his own opinion, explaining "with regret" his reasons for ruling against the plaintiff.

"Even though we lost, it was mollifying to receive an explanation," the attorney for the plaintiff remarked.

This promises to be one book you *can* judge by its cover. (MS)

Spa! (July 16, 2002)

"It's circumcised, weighs 350 kilograms, is made of wood at least 200 years old and is shaped exactly how the ideal penis should be," Kenshu Ikeda tells *Spa!* referring to the two-meter-long male member that is the showpiece of the Tagata Shrine in Komaki, Aichi Prefecture, where he acts as chief priest. "What people have to remember, though, is that this shrine is not for those looking to improve their sexual prowess. There are so many people out there whose earnest desire for a child cannot be met."

Though most Japanese will insist they are not religious, Buddhism and Shinto are still deeply rooted in the lives of most people across the country. Nearly all homes have a Buddhist altar and it's common for businesses to set up portable shrines to pray for success. Some Buddhist temples or Shinto shrines, though, exist to meet special needs.

Tagata Jinja is a case in point. Aside from its world famous festival in March where locals take out the male member and parade it through the streets, a normal day at Tagata Jinja attracts believers worried about their failure to bear children, those whose fertility treatment has failed or sperm count is too low. Shrine officials say many have their wish granted. "I suppose some mysterious power must be at work," Ikeda says.

Kanayama Jinja Shrine in Kawasaki plays a similar role. Its grounds contain myriad phallic statues adorned with votive tablets written by followers whose fears about fornication give them the willies.

"Craftsmen who used fire or iron during the Edo Period (1603–

1868) had a deep belief in the god Kanayama. People soon made the link between tools that spark fire and harmony among couples," the shrine's chief priestess Kimiko Nakamura tells the magazine. "The shrine is said to answer the prayers of those seeking lots of offspring and the prevention of venereal diseases. It's also said to ward off AIDS and ensure the success of sex change operations."

Kinchu-ji Temple in Kyoto specializes in getting couples together in the first place. Young women throng to the temple on weekend mornings to hear mantras prayed that will provide them with an ever-binding connection to whatever their heart desires.

"We don't mind if believers wish for two or three things at the same time," Chief Priest Shogen Katsura says. "Eventually, the object desired most will come true. And, when it does come true, we welcome people to come back again and ask for something more."

While Kinchu-ji Temple aims to get people together with what they want most, Yasui Konpiramiya Shrine in Kyoto promises followers a clean break from whatever is plaguing them, be that cigarettes, tobacco, but mostly partners. Middle-aged women pray for trouble-free divorces and plenty of alimony, while younger women implore for respite from the attention of stalkers and fathers beg for daughters to find a better guy than the one they've already got.

"We get all sorts here," says Chief Priest Hajime Torii. "Even the selfish types like those girls who ask for a couple to break up so they can have the guy to themselves."

Other shrines focus on help of a different kind. Shiramine Jingu Shrine in Kyoto is said to be the birthplace of *kemari*, an ancient game resembling soccer that was played among Shinto priests. The shrine is the only place that deifies the god of sports.

"Sports involve competition. If there is a winner, there must be a loser," the shrine's Shigeyuki Kitamura tells *Spa!* "Praying at our shrine takes the pain out of losing. Still, we have had many teams and famous players thank us for answering their prayers." (RC)

CONSUMER ZOMBIES MUST BUY

Spa! (August 6, 2002)

When Masami Handa was little, she spent hours watching while her mother indulged in manicures. Now she's 32, works for an ad agency, and finds herself uncontrollably hooked—to the point that nearly a fourth of her salary each month goes into nail polish and nail care products.

"I usually buy about 30 bottles a month, spending ¥50,000 out of a take-home pay of ¥200,000," she confesses to *Spa!* "If I'm forced to choose between a meal and a manicure, I'll choose the latter." At least Handa understands she's in the throes of an obsession. "Sure, I regret what I do," she admits. "I'll say to myself, 'Oh darn, I've bought the same color again.' But when I see a new product, I've absolutely got to have it."

How much nail polish can one person possibly acquire? By Handa's own estimate, over the past 10 years she's laid out ¥10 *million* for the little bottles—the equivalent of 500 round trip tickets on the Bullet Train between Tokyo and Nagoya.

Then there's 29-year-old Junichi Nakagawa, who works for a TV production company. Television, it seems, gives to Nakagawa with one hand and takes away with the other. He's hopelessly addicted to telemarketing. "As soon as I see them flash 'Limited to 30 customers!' on the screen, I leap for the phone," he says. "Once I ordered a pressure cooker. And I don't even cook at home."

A sucker for fitness goods, Nakagawa also purchased, in quick succession, an Airwalker exercise machine and Abtronic massage belt. If his residence had more space for the items he so compulsively orders, he would have almost certainly spent more than the roughly ¥1 million he's laid out over the past seven years. But even that figure is sufficient to pay for a *gyudon* (beef over rice) lunch at Yoshinoya every day for an entire decade.

Despite this addiction, Nakagawa should be grateful. His outlays are but a small fraction—$\frac{1}{20}$ or so—of what poor Kazuki Mochida, 37, has dispensed for computer hardware over the past decade. His first acquisition was an Apple IIci, equipped with a then blazing-fast 2,400 bps modem. Since then, he's been acquiring PCs at the rate of one or two a year. He currently owns eight, but confesses that he "probably doesn't really need that many."

"Sometimes I feel a little self-conscious after I buy the latest model," Mochida admits. "But if I deny myself, the stress is palpable. I'm completely hooked."

Whether fashion-related or high-tech, any genre susceptible to rapid obsolescence has a pool of potential customers who can be mesmerized into acquiring as much, or as many, as they can afford. *Spa!* cites cell phones and the never-ending assortment of digital goodies as the most popular items, along with designer handbags—which one young woman snatches up to the tune of about 30 a year—¥1.2 million worth.

"We're not collectors, since a collector doesn't use the things he buys, but adorns his home or puts them on display," says Tsukasa Seki, a technical writer for popular publications.

Haruka Koishihara, author of *Starbucks Maniacs*, agrees. "There's something solitary about what we do," she notes. "There are some aspects of collecting in our acquisitiveness, but the sense of satisfaction is much cooler than that felt by a fervid hobbyist. It's more like . . . being driven by a desire for pure ownership."

The magazine concludes—only half in jest—that more of these "slaves" might be just the thing Japan needs to jump-start its flagging economy. (MS)

VIDEO GAMERS GO MAD

Shukan Bunshun (September 26, 2002)

It's called "game brain," and it can turn youngsters into violent, antisocial monsters. So says Akio Mori, who has just released a book on this form of dementia, which he claims is caused by the prolonged playing of electronic games, and *Shukan Bunshun* reports on his findings.

In a nutshell, his research on some 350 people aged three to 30 has found that habitual video and computer gaming can eventually lead to a permanent loss of brain-wave functions. That in turn can lead to shortened concentration spans, sudden bursts of anger and losses of basic social skills.

The study, explained in Dr. Mori's book, *Gemu No no Kyofu* (Terror of Game Brain), focuses on the beta waves that shoot around our brain's frontal lobe. This part of the brain is its control tower, where a human's creative and rational impulses originate, and the beta waves are an indicator of the brain's activity. "Brain waves known as beta waves are produced when the brain is active. That allows us to examine activities within the frontal lobe," Mori tells the magazine.

When test subjects who were habitual gamers became immersed in their gaming, their beta waves dropped by varying amounts, from only slight declines to complete loss, the study found. The degree of change depended on how serious a gamer the subject was.

A test group made up of people who spent moderate amounts of time in front of their game monitors experienced normal levels of beta waves at the start of their sessions. Their waves dropped after three or four hours of play. Once they stopped playing, however, their frontal-lobe activity returned to normal.

But the brains of hardcore gamers—those who play from two to seven hours daily—showed frightening results: Their beta waves were constantly near zero, even when they weren't gaming, according to Mori. Hence his term "game brain."

By contrast, members of the "normal" group of subjects—those who rarely ever played the games—experienced no loss in beta waves whether they were playing the games or not.

The research also examined the brain activity of people who type e-mail on cell phones or watch horror movies. A similar pattern emerged, with beta waves declining depending on the person's history of e-mail use or exposure to the movies.

So what's wrong with depleted beta waves?

"When the frontal lobe suffers from significant drops of activity, the circulation of blood there worsens, causing it to degenerate," says Mori, a professor at Nihon University. He recounts a "typical case of game brain" —an 8-year-old boy who has been gaming constantly since he was 18 months old.

"When he plays the games, he froths at the mouth, and when he loses he goes off the deep end, often throwing the game device around," he says. "His parents have taken him to be checked at a hospital eight times although there's never been any sign of epilepsy."

Atsuko Kusanagi, a journalist who last year published a book on the supposed link between electronic games and juvenile crime, believes that Mori's findings are a serious matter of concern. "I think it took a lot of courage to release the results—which are critical of TV games—in Japan, a world leader when it comes to electronic games," she says. (GB)

Shukan Shincho (December 19, 2002)

Except for his long hair that looks as though it's never been cut, he could pass as any other young man. His looks suggest he could only be Japanese. He grew up in Kanagawa Prefecture. Yet he barely speaks the local lingo. Instead, his English is nearly flawless. Some call him Ken, but even he doesn't know if that's his real name.

There is, as *Shukan Shincho* notes, something far more irregular about this chap than merely the extraordinarily harsh penalty the Yokohama District Court handed him on December 5 upon a conviction for theft and trespassing.

"He has no family register, so naturally he does not have citizenship. From the time of his arrest, through his indictment and during his trial, he has been referred to as 'Stateless Person Calling Himself A.' He says he's 24, but we only have his word for it. He claims his parents are Japanese, but he doesn't know who they are or where they came from. He can speak a little Japanese, but usually uses English. He had to have an interpreter through his court case," a reporter on the court beat says.

Family registers form the basis of most Japanese' official lives. Like, say social security numbers, family registers are needed for nearly every aspect of life in Japan.

"Stateless Person Calling Himself A," or "Ken," or whatever, whoever, he is, found himself in trouble with the police on the afternoon of September 4. He went to the Naka Municipal Government offices in Yokohama to talk to social welfare officials there. While the welfare officer wasn't looking, the mystery man suddenly snatched some documents and ran away.

"Those documents outlined what he'd told us about himself on previous visits he'd made to the office. They contained information about his personal details," a government official tells a reporter. "I chased after him, but he ran into a locker room, locked the door and wouldn't come out again. After a while, the police came along and used a skeleton key to open the room. He'd ripped up all the documents he stole."

As the man's court case progressed through November, the mystery of his upbringing slowly started to become apparent. "He says that he lived with a family on the U.S. Yokosuka Naval Base until he was 13. He can't remember anything before that. He has no idea if his parents simply dumped him. On the base, everybody referred to him as 'Ken.' When the American couple who'd been looking after him were redeployed Stateside, he started living at Yamate, a small facility detached from the main base," the court rounds hack says.

"Ken" struggled to get by in the real world. He sought help at a Christian church in Yokohama, where he became acquainted with a Japanese priest. He later adopted the priest's surname, but couldn't stay at the church for long. He kept in touch with the priest, but was basically homeless.

"In 1998, the priest said he'd look after him and introduced him to the officials at Naka Municipal Government so he could go about getting welfare and he even borrowed an apartment. He promised he'd try and get onto a family register, but ended up getting a puppy, which caused the landlord to boot him out of the apartment where he was staying. He never showed any real inclination to go about getting a family register and his welfare payments ran out in February," the reporter tells *Shukan Shincho*.

All that "Ken" stole were the documents from city hall. "I only took them because I thought that if there was no way I could get official help, I would take my records and see what the private sector could do for me. He told the court the reason why he didn't try to get a family register, was because he was sick of all the people telling him to go to school or get citizenship when he was already having enough trouble trying to find something to eat and a place to live," Ken's lawyer tells the magazine. "To be honest, when I first heard his story, I thought he was making it up. But he's told exactly the same story to his priest buddy and welfare officials. Everything he's saying is true. I think it's vital that we go about trying to create an environment that will allow him to ease into society." (RC)

THEY SAID IT IN THE *Weeklies*

"The language is somewhat extreme, with words that don't occur in our everyday conversation. I won't say there is no embarrassment."

—Hikari Osawa, on the problem of finding women for her business— recording audio versions of pornographic novels for the blind—to *Aera* (November 8, 2003)

WALKMAN KICKS STOWAWAY'S ASS

dacapo (February 19, 2003)

Melty Kiss. Sweat. Pocky. What gooey, goofy environment begot these syllables? And attached them to consumer products—a chocolate treat, a drink and a chocolate-topped stick-shaped biscuit, respectively? And expected them to sell? And was right?

A product name is a mysterious thing, *dacapo* finds. It can be as blandly descriptive as "Green Gum," as lovely, if meaningless, as "Saran," and as devoid of meaning and beauty alike . . . as "Walkman." Walkman—therein hangs a tale.

When Sony's portable tape player debuted in 1979 it was called Stowaway in the U.K. and Soundabout in the U.S. Both names yielded to the drab pidgin-English Walkman, its Japanese appellation. Now you can look Walkman up in some dictionaries and find it defined, a mere name no longer.

This next story takes us back to 1958, when Japanese product naming was a prosaic matter of identifying the merchandise. Haguromo Foods' Sea Chicken (an unacknowledged variation of the American "Chicken of the Sea") broke the mold. Sea chicken? What on earth was that? At first, sales of the canned tuna went nowhere; the idea of an imaginative product name was ahead of its time. But—thanks in no small measure, *dacapo* says, to the cute cartoon "sea chicken" that starred in the ads—the times soon caught up, and sales rocketed.

What's in a name? Product success or failure, that's what. In 1985 Itoen surmounted numerous technical difficulties to produce the world's first canned green tea. Its name was Kan-iri Sencha—Canned

Green Tea—and it flopped. In 1989, the name was changed to Oi-ocha, derived from "Oi! Ocha!"—a husband's curt but typical demand to his wife for a cup of tea. Sales soared.

Is there a pattern? A standard? Euphony, one might think—but Walkman? The message, perhaps—but Pocky? On second thought, maybe Glico did have a message in mind when it dreamed up Pocky. It comes, the magazine says, from *pokkin*—not a word but a sound, the sound the stick-biscuit makes when bitten.

"Ad budgets are shrinking," explains an analyst the magazine consults. "If you can't advertise a product, the name itself must be the advertisement. It has to have instant impact."

If a random survey of your neighborhood convenience store turns up names wackier than most, the reason is clear. Convenience store cash registers keep track of what items sell and what items don't. Those that don't are swept out—no appeal, no second chance. If your product name is selling your product, you better make it good.

Many sound-names are word fusions, some ingenious, some tortured. AIBO, the dog-robot that went on sale in 1999, comes from AI, artificial intelligence, and a slice of the second syllable of "robot." Cray-pas is "crayon" plus "pastel." Kobayashi Pharmaceutical's intestinal medicine Gaspitan pairs intestinal "gas" with "*pitan* (quick stop)."

For years, Japan's top-selling car was Toyota's Corolla, suggesting flower petals. In 2002 it was overtaken by Honda's Fit, suggesting . . . what, exactly? Fitness? Fits?

Fuji Film's disposable cameras looked like cardboard boxes. "*Honto ni utsuru no?*—Does this thing actually take pictures?" a skeptical customer might ask. The affirmative answer became the product name: "Utsuru'n *desu.*"

As with product names, so with corporate logos. Staid is out, cute is in. Would you trust your savings to a bank named Tomato? When

Sanyo Sogo Bank became the Tomato Bank in 1989, it seemed a bit flaky—but people were growing tired of the solid but chilly dependability conveyed by traditional names. Depositors laughed and gave it their blessings. So now you've got banks with names like Sakura (cherry blossom) and Mizuho (vigorous rice plants).

Well, why not? It's harmless, fun, in tune with the times. With subatomic particles sporting names like strawberry quark, why shouldn't a bank call itself Tomato? Or a drink, Sweat? Or a magazine, *dacapo*? (MH)

THEY SAID IT IN THE *Weeklies*

"I once passed out after taking 100 pills. However, wrist cuts cause less damage and don't ruin your status at school as much."

—Sumire, one of the "gothic Lolita" teenagers who hang out in trendy Harajuku, about flirting with suicide to *Aera* (July 12, 2004)

■ ■ ■

"It doesn't mean I want to die. I like myself, and I want to get involved in a band or something."

—16-year-old "gothic Lolita" Izuri, who admits enjoying viewing photos of dead bodies and reading the *Complete Manual of Suicide*, in the same magazine

BAR PATRONS PAY TO BREATHE

Shukan Gendai (April 12, 2003)

From a distance, the Wing Oxy Bar in the Tenjinbashi district of Osaka looks like just another trendy bar or cafe. Yet take a closer look and you'll find that the customers, instead of holding beer or whiskey glasses or cups of coffee, have plastic tubes running up their noses. Look even closer and some will probably have a euphoric expression on their faces.

The customers are here to suck in concentrated amounts of oxygen, which they believe does the body a world of good, from curing stress and fatigue, to shedding unwanted weight, to improving blood circulation. On top of all that, they say, the oxygen fix feels really, really good.

Beneath the counter at Oxy Wing are oxygen concentrators/generators, machines that produce air that is 90 percent oxygen (normal air is about 20 percent). These are connected to infusers, clear bottles containing liquids of various colors. The liquids are aromatic and as the bottles' name suggests, they infuse the air with herbal or fruity aromas of one's choice. After passing through liquids, the enriched air travels through the tubes, and is deposited into the customers' nostrils.

Customers buy their own tubes, called nasal cannula, the type used in hospitals, for ¥300 a piece. Ten minutes of breathing the enriched air cost ¥500, 20 minutes ¥900–1,000, and 30 minutes ¥1,200.

The owner of Wing Oxy, Seigo Sano, got the idea of setting up the bar after visiting the United States, where they first appeared several years ago. "When I went to Las Vegas two-and-a-half years ago, I spotted a place about eight tsubo [about 26 sq. meters] in a shopping mall that turned out to be an oxygen bar," he says. "In this day and age, it costs money to drink water, so it seems we've also reached a point where we pay to breathe air."

Not that Sano's customers mind having to fork out cash for the most abundant element on Earth. Since opening a little over a year ago, business has been booming and more than 1,900 members have signed up. What's more, there are plans to sell Wing Oxy franchises to operators elsewhere in Japan.

To figure out whether all this is just hype, *Shukan Gendai* dispatches a 54-year-old reporter, who suffers from stress and fatigue. Once at the bar, he deeply inhales concentrated oxygen scented with lavender. His first sense is that the air has filled every nook and cranny of his lungs.

After about 10 minutes, he feels a warmth in his fingertips. This, he figures, is a sign of improved circulation, one of the purported health benefits of breathing the enriched air. The reporter's head feels distinctly clear and sharp. After 20 minutes, he removes the nasal cannula only to realize that his fatigue has all but disappeared. And the warmth in his fingertips lingers for an hour afterward.

Many of the other customers in the bar the magazine talks with are professionals working in demanding fields, such as IT and design. They are there to counter stress and ailments they've developed at their workplaces. And most, it should be pointed out, are repeat customers. (GB)

WACKY CLUBS ENTICE WACKY FOLK

Flash (May 27, 2003)

In a Japan that demands conformity, individuality is usually performed in groups. And some of Japan's wackiest clubs tend to attract some of the country's most, well, interesting individuals, as *Flash* reveals.

Take *Kiri no Kai*, a collection of devotees who worship the beauty of images of kimono-clad women committing hara-kiri. In the past, members of the club with a 20-year-long history, held mock *seppuku* (formal hara-kiri) sessions, but now its activities are largely centered on the annual newsletter.

Also concerning traditional Japanese beauty is the *Iga-ryu Ninjutsu Fuko Hozon Kai* (Association for the Restoration and Preservation of the Iga School of Ninjutsu), a group of about 200 women who pretend to be *kunoichi*, female ninja. Events are held up to seven times a year, when the mostly teen or 20-something members gather together in their ninja outfits and exchange secret techniques or meet with like-minded ninja fans. A notable feature of the club is that members are only ever known by their ninja names and true identities must never be revealed.

For a more modern approach, there's Tokyo-based Studio Grace, which has managed to attract some 40 members, among them 14 female models aged from 19 to 26 who'll willingly adopt any pose requested by male shutterbugs. Usually, the models will wear one of the roughly 30 costumes the club possesses, running from a policewoman to a racing queen. "Most of the time, the guys want us to pose so we show off a flash of our undies or bra," one of the models says.

Along similar lines is Leg-Smith, whose 20 women models share the common trait of a decent set of legs that they will gladly allow fetishists to snap away at with their cameras—provided that any shots taken are strictly below the belt.

Another for those with slightly different tastes is *Pansuto* (Pantyhose) Fetish Club, whose 100 members take great pride in wearing full body suits covering them from head to toe. The club meets once a month, with members required to turn up clad in their body hugging costumes.

For those into hugging and costumes, it's hard to go past Baby Mate. The roughly 500-member ensemble enjoys biannual camps on the Izu Peninsula where male members return to the days of their infancy, sucking on pacifiers and wearing diapers. Really lucky toddlers get a special breast-feeding, while bad boys who dirty themselves can also look forward to getting a change from sympathetic mommy types.

Schoolgirls are all the go for those enrolled in *Himawari Gakuen Joshi Koto Gakko* (Sunflower Girls High School), whose all-male entourage takes great pleasure in decking themselves out as schoolgirls for events held four to five times a year. Uniform-clad members ride trains and travel around the streets in groups while pursuing such pastimes as shopping or even trips. Special camps offer orientation courses for beginners embarrassed at the prospect of wearing a schoolgirl uniform in public.

Perhaps taking the image of the giggling schoolgirl a step further is the *Pai Nage Kurabu* (Pie Chuckers' Club). This gaggle of gals from all walks of life originally started as a pie-baking group, but instead now gather together several times a month to hurl the pies they bake at each other, covering themselves in pastry and whipped cream in no time at all.

"We used to record TV shows where people threw pies at each other and then assembled to watch the footage together. In the end, though, we decided we'd rather throw the pies at ourselves," one of the members tells *Flash*. Men are also welcomed into the club, provided they intend to bake and hurl their own pies. For those living outside of Tokyo who'd like a slice of the pie, so to speak, the group sells videos of their gatherings.

Considering how filthy members would get, perhaps they may enroll in the *Konyoku Kurabu* (Mixed Bathing Club), a group dedicated to traversing the archipelago in search of hot spring resorts where men and women can bathe together in the buff. Touching is strictly prohibited among the mostly 20 and 30-something membership, who have official meetings two to three times a year, but arrange any number of side-trips among themselves at other times. The club's website features a host of photos of club trips.

Some would argue that those caught up in these clubs should be shot. If so, what better place to contact than the Japan Rubber Band Shooting Association? The group has a membership of around 400 whose ages range from elementary school pupils to grannies in their 80s, all of who have a liking for shooting elastic bands from their handmade guns. The association even holds national tournaments to determine Japan's best rubber band sharpshooters.

"If you practice your shooting," an association member helpfully tells *Flash*, "there's no doubt you'll improve." (RC)

MEDIA PINS
ANGRY WRESTLER

Various (June, 2003)

Back in the 13th century, the Mongol armies of Genghis Khan didn't overrun a good part of the civilized world by being nice guys. But in this day and age, where looting and plundering have given way to admission-ticket sales and TV-commercial endorsements as a source of income, tough-as-nails Mongolians in professional sumo are expected to adhere to the same gentlemanly rules as their Japanese counterparts.

The day after Mongolian *yokozuna* (grand champion) Asashoryu's 13-win, 2-loss victorious slate in the summer grand sumo tournament, three weeklies appeared with articles critical of his unsportsmanlike behavior, both inside and outside the straw ring.

The worst of Asashoryu's transgressions by far was broadcast nationwide by NHK TV. In the match against his compatriot, veteran wrestler Kyokushuzan, on the ninth day of the tournament, the heretofore undefeated Asashoryu, aged 22, was pulled off balance and hit the dirt a fraction of a second before he pushed Kyokushuzan out of the straw ring. When the referee gave the nod to Kyokushuzan, Asashoryu broke with tradition by facing the head judge and gesturing to dispute the call. He then angrily swung his *sagari* tassels and brushed shoulders with his opponent as they passed in midring. Finally he stormed back to the dressing room, flinging off his tape bindings and repeatedly cursing out loud.

It gets worse. A sports writer tells *Shukan Post* he heard from Kyokushuzan that before leaving the ring, Asashoryu also spat out the Mongol epithet *"pizda"* —the equivalent of a four-letter expletive not fit to print in a family newspaper. (Or even, apparently, in the *Post*.)

The magazine goes on to supply a detailed list of Asashoryu's other transgressions, which range from acts of cruelty toward junior wrestlers in his stable, damaging a dressing-room ceiling-fan cover when he angrily kicked off his straw sandal following a loss at the Osaka tournament last March, to insisting on his own hairdresser. He also allegedly addressed a Korean sportswriter as *"Kimchi yaro* (you kimchi-eating bastard)!"

Shukan Tokuho reports that Asashoryu's womanizing has become notorious since he won the Kyushu tournament in November. In Osaka in March, he requested a nightclub hostess to sleep with him and when she demurely refused, he reached into a bag beside him and plopped ¥10 million in cold cash on the table to sweeten the offer. As the story has it, the woman politely stood her ground.

More than just winning bouts, remarks *Shukan Tokuho*, a yokozuna is expected to exemplify the sport through a personal quality called *hinkaku* (outstanding decorum or composure). Asashoryu's loutish behavior, it huffs, shows he's unworthy of his exalted ranking.

Nor have Asashoryu's peccadillos escaped the notice of the Yokozuna Deliberation Council, the group of bigwigs entrusted with advising the Sumo Association on promotions to the sport's highest rank. *Shukan Taishu* reports that some council members have even gone so far as to mull his demotion from the rank.

Sumo's declining popularity, for whatever reason, was reflected in the nearly 3,500 unsold tickets on the third day of the just-ended tournament. Where complete daily sellouts were once typical, even choice *masu-seki* (box seats) at the Kokugikan arena went unoccupied on some days.

Is sumo's decline irreversible? Some cynics are now even going so far as to suggest that Japan's national sport ought to take a cue from pro wrestling and harness Asashoryu's bad-boy behavior to its advantage. "Actually, having him play the guy in the black hat is not necessarily a bad way to go," *manga* cartoonist Yasuyuki Kunitomo tells *Shukan Taishu*. "The problem is, right now there's no 'baby face' Japanese wrestler to give him a proper thrashing.

"From the standpoint of popularity, ability and personal character, *ozeki* (champion) Tochiazuma would be the ideal candidate. If he can make it to yokozuna and then give Asashoryu a solid drubbing in the ring, I'm sure sumo's popularity would pick up again." (MS)

THEY SAID IT IN THE *Weeklies*

"The human market has just about peaked."

—Professional astrologer to *Shukan Asahi* (August 1, 2003) about the increasing number of reports of pets being possessed by spirits

VOODOO CURSES MADE TO ORDER

dacapo (July 2, 2003)

It's all serious business at the Japan Voodoo Association, where clients are treated with the utmost care and attention.

"You can speak with the *sensei* after we've confirmed that your payment has been successfully transferred," says the velvety voice on the other end of the association's toll-free line. Through the "association," which is really a business, customers can arrange to have curses put on their worst enemies. This involves a spooky and elaborate ceremony headed by a sorcerer who mutilates a *wara ningyo*, a traditional Japanese straw doll which, of course, serves nicely as a voodoo doll.

The business of calling up the spirits to wreck the lives of others is booming these days, association representative Junichiro Kisaragi tells *dacapo*. "Each month we handle about 30 to 40 new cases," he says, adding that nearly all his revenge-seeking clients are women in their 30s and 40s.

What's more, the vast majority of these women are in a common predicament: They've had their lover stolen away from them and are bent on destroying the woman responsible.

Kisaragi produces one customer's hand-written letter, which outlines a typical scenario. Miss A, who's in her 30s, was madly, although secretly, in love with a much younger male coworker, Mr. B. One day she confronted him to confess her love. But what she didn't know was that Mr. B had already been seeing Miss C and had just gotten her pregnant. The happy young couple registered their marriage shortly thereafter.

Mr. B then proceeded to ignore the attentions of Miss A, leaving her emotionally shattered. That's when she decided to consult the voodoo specialists.

Her curse reads: "To Miss C: You are a coward who purposely got pregnant so you could have Mr. B for yourself. I will not allow this. I will not allow the birth of Mr. B's child." The solution to her problem, as she saw it, was to stick tacks into the middle section of a straw doll representing the allegedly conniving Miss C, in the hope of terminating the pregnancy.

Such an approach, according to Kisaragi, can have a high likelihood of success. Of course, it largely depends on how much money the client is willing to fork out. "It's about an 80 percent [rate of success] for the ¥50,000 program, 70 percent for the ¥30,000 program and 50 percent for the ¥15,000 program," he boasts.

For those who want to do it themselves, or those who can't be bothered to make it out deep into the woods where the rituals are performed, the association sells voodoo "sets." These contain all the paraphernalia necessary to ensure at least a decent chance that the grisliest of curses are played out. Apart from the straw doll, there's a rope, a pin and some tacks, along with a hammer to bang them in.

"If you hammer the tacks into the wara ningyo's feet, then [your enemy's] feet will have problems. In the chest, and the organs go bad," Kisaragi says, rather matter-of-factly. (GB)

GHOSTLY KILLER PENS HORROR STORY

Friday (August 15, 2003)

Summer is the season of ghostly encounters. That's because the spirits of the dead choose this time of year to return briefly to Earth, according to Japanese legend.

In keeping with this ghoulish tradition, the weeklies are in the habit of detailing the country's most haunted locations in their August editions. *Friday* picks eight such places and accords each with a "scariness" rating of between one and five, as indicated by skull-and-cross-bone icons.

Judging by the article, Saitama Prefecture is an especially scary place, as three of the eight haunted spots are located here. One such location is along the highway connecting the prefecture to Tokyo's Ikebukuro district. As with the other seven spots, the area's name is not given, presumably so as not to anger the local authorities who fear the negative publicity that residents of the netherworld might attract to their locale.

Still, readers are told it's at the point on the highway where a forest begins to appear. Push through the trees and you'll suddenly be confronted by a looming tower attached to what appears to be a crumbling European castle. The building was, in fact, a love hotel, although these days it's dark, empty and abandoned.

According to the locals, a hotel guest murdered his lover about 10 years ago, leaving the walls of their room splattered with blood. Repeated attempts to paint over the stains had no effect—they just kept resurfacing. They remain there to this day.

What's more, in the aftermath of the killing local residents told of an apparition of the dead woman wandering the hotel's corridors. The widespread rumor was enough to deter amorous couples from checking in, and the hotel's owner was forced to close the place down for lack of business. Nowadays, people who try to enter the building don't stick around long: Once inside they are confronted by the ghost, who reportedly has blood dripping from her left eye and stares silently at the intruders.

But the scariest place of all, with a rating of five skulls and crossbones, is a residential area of Tokyo.

Years ago, an elderly woman brutally killed all four members of her family here. A court found her insane, so she was sent to a mental hospital rather than imprisoned. But she returned to the house several years later, from which time she became obsessed with her murderous rampage. Perhaps as a catharsis, she recalled the events by writing them out in lengthy detail on numerous pages that she stuck on the exterior walls, doors and anywhere else around the house. One reads, "The organs flew right out when I stabbed with the knife."

Neighbors say that for years they have been hearing strange sounds and the voices of several people emanating from inside the empty house. The faded pages remain stuck to the walls.

Among *Friday*'s other scary spots are a cave in Shizuoka Prefecture where nearby motorists report seeing a samurai's face in their rearview mirrors; a wooded area in Osaka Prefecture that was an execution ground for criminals in the Edo Period; and a road in Hyogo Prefecture where frequently spotted ghosts are believed to be behind an inordinate number of accidents in a local tunnel.

It's enough to add an ominous chill to the hottest summer weather. (GB)

SHAME LOST, SOCIETY SUFFERS

dacapo (August 20, 2003)

"Whenever I hear the word 'shame,'" writes social critic Keiko Higuchi in *dacapo*, " I think of a scene I witnessed 25 years ago." A small child on a train was obnoxiously blocking the doorway. "Be careful," said the child's mother. "You'll hurt yourself."

Not "you're in people's way," or "you're being a nuisance," but a purely self-centered admonition that does nothing to direct the child's attention to the rights or even the existence of others. "That," says Higuchi, "may be our biggest problem. We no longer see other people."

Shame is *dacapo*'s theme—shamelessness, rather. "Somehow," the magazine declares, "Japan has become a shameless country." If that's true, it's a revolution; a radical departure from the refined taste and dignified restraint that marked Japan's traditional culture. You can lament the loss, or, with equal validity, celebrate the freedom gained. As advertising analyst Yukichi Amano notes in his contribution to the article, "It's not always a bad thing to outgrow yesterday's inhibitions."

No, but Amano himself can't help squirming at the phony exuberance—"anarchy," he calls it—prevailing on television. True, he concedes, the mindless shopping programs may be useful to consumers, and the gossipy talk shows, though generally rambling and inconsequential, do reflect the "hodgepodge" of crude daily reality; still, he says, "TV nowadays is pretty strange." Is its rejection of aesthetic restraint a reflection of social trends, or a cause of them?

"There are two kinds of rules," observes Kunio Suzuki, founder of the neorightist group Issuikai, "society's rules, and club rules or peer-group rules." The former embody stern, no-nonsense common sense—what parents should be teaching their children. Club rules can embody anything at all (Waseda University's Super-Free date-rape club had rules that can land those obeying them in jail). Young women painting their toenails on a train might draw frowns (which they ostentatiously ignore), but their comportment falls quite within the bounds, such as they are, set by their peers.

"When group rules overwhelm society's rules," Suzuki writes, "you have the makings of a shameless country."

The root problem, in his view, is anonymity. "The Japanese seem to feel that in a group you can get away with anything. You become like the invisible man," he says. "I, myself, was like that when I was involved in radical rightwing politics, barking slogans from a sound-truck loudspeaker. That, too, was a kind of anonymity."

Modern mass society has carried anonymity to extremes beyond all historical precedent. Parents and children drift past each other and don't look back. "In the past, parents took care to behave in such a way that their children would not be ashamed of them," says Higuchi. "Today, it seems, the only parental responsibility is to lavish money on their children's education. How the parents live is not considered relevant."

Then, adds Suzuki, there is that postmodern agora of anonymity, the Internet, where "invisible man" ceases to be a metaphor. "You can post any kind of nonsense on an Internet bulletin board," he says. "You can buy and sell drugs, guns. You can slander people. And all the while you're perfectly, unchallengeably anonymous."

And when did politics reach its present nadir? In 1994, says analyst Minoru Morita, when the Social Democratic Party became the Liberal Democratic Party's partner in power, reversing at a cynical stroke 40 years of left-wing, idealistic oppositional politics. Cynicism is corrosive. Shame is defenseless against it. (MH)

On July 25, 2003, attorneys representing the Japan Public Highway Corporation and its president, Haruho Fujii, filed suit in the Tokyo District Court, demanding publisher Bungei Shunju and Sachio Katagiri, deputy head of the highway corporation's Shikoku Regional Bureau, pay ¥30 million in damages.

The plaintiffs claimed that Katagiri's expose article in the monthly magazine *Bungei Shunju*, titled "Exposing the Lies and Tyranny of Japan Highway President Fujii," constituted libel. The article accused the corporation of concealing liabilities of ¥617.5 billion in last year's financial statements, showing close to ¥5.8 trillion in net assets instead.

The article appeared at an acutely sensitive time, as reformers are in the process of debating privatization of the corporation.

"The media was doing what it was supposed to be doing, which is running down a story and determining the truth of the allegations," asserts Kimio Tsuji, an attorney and director of the public-support group Public Interest Speak-up Advisers. "If there's a strong likelihood that the information is factual, it is ludicrous to sue for libel."

If libel cases seldom made news in the past, it was mainly because courts had been stingy in awarding claims. But in March 2001, publisher Shogakukan was ordered to cough up what was then the most generous settlement ever awarded—¥10 million—to Yomiuri Giants infielder Kazuhiro Kiyohara. The figure was later pared to ¥6 million upon appeal; but perhaps encouraged by

Kiyohara's success, others converged on the courts, upping the size of claims, with some demanding hundreds of millions in damages.

Sunday Mainichi lists 33 major libel lawsuits filed against book, magazine and newspaper publishers since March 2002. Some are pending; the most exorbitant claim, by a hospital in Kumamoto Prefecture, demanded publisher Shinchosha pay a whopping ¥583.7 million. The plaintiff has since been awarded ¥23.1 million and Shinchosha was ordered to run a retraction and apology.

"Standards for legal judgments are not absolute, but change according to the mores of the times," explains Shinichiro Fujioka, editor of the analytical journal Sogo Journalism Studies. "Society's stance on journalistic ethics seems to have become more demanding."

So it appears. When delivering his verdict against magazine publisher Kobunsha, a Tokyo District Court judge remarked, "The magazine ran the article with the object of gaining profits; unless obliged to pay significant compensation it cannot be expected to refrain from similar illegal acts in the future."

Hideo Shimizu, professor emeritus of Aoyama Gakuin University and a director of media watchdog organization The Information Clearinghouse Japan, finds this attitude worrisome. "Maybe the media's not always right, and needs to do a better job of verifying what it prints; but for the law to make a simple judgment that a piece is 'profit-seeking sensationalism' is a real problem," he says. "The law must always accept the constitutional right to freedom of expression. Otherwise the existence of our free, democratic society might very well be threatened." (MS)

STRIP DIPLOMACY MELTS NORTH KOREAN ICE

Shukan Post (October 10, 2003)

Ai Aoyama, a former Ginza hostess and sado-masochism queen, has led a rather wild and glamorous life. During her career, she has charmed and also whipped some of Japan's most famous politicians and entertainers.

But since retiring, she has developed a philanthropic streak, which includes a keen desire to help the starving masses in North Korea. To that end, she has traveled to the Hermit Kingdom not once, but twice, the most recent trip taking place last month, according to *Shukan Post*.

She says that during her stays, she has been wined and dined by some of the country's highest-ranking officials, including one who attended the historic summit between Prime Minister Junichiro Koizumi and North Korean leader Kim Jong Il. All treated her with the utmost kindness and consideration. "North Korea has this scary image but when you meet the local people that's not the case," Aoyama says.

The goal of her visits was to help deliver food and other forms of assistance. One of her destinations was an orphanage housing 20 to 30 kids aged three and four. "We delivered powdered milk, crayons, drawing paper and toys. But I regretted not being able to give the items to the children directly," she says.

However, her activities in the reclusive country have not been limited to charity work. From the day she touched down, the straight-laced Stalinists invited her out to party almost every night. "After dinner on the first night, a bunch of the top-ranking people said they were going to have a 'meeting,'" says Aoyama. "The place was the karaoke pub in my hotel. It turned out to be a really wild time."

What ensued were lively renditions of some famous Japanese songs, accompanied by "hip-shaking bellydancing," Aoyama recalls. And it turned out to be the perfect setting for Aoyama to practice her own special brand of citizen-diplomacy. "My specialty is surprising people, like throwing myself against my partner's chest," she explains. "You get a big response when you do things like 'accidently' show a bit of nudity or, instead of just saying 'hello' to a guy, you squeeze an important part of his body.

"That's how to open people's hearts ... and build relationships."

She managed to open the heart of one stodgy communist who was sitting beside her at a drinking session. "I put 'the grip' on him and he said, 'Whoah!' But then the atmosphere became extremely free and relaxed. The guy said, 'Ms. Aoyama, you really are a funny person.'"

It was during the same party that the vivacious Japanese visitor managed to live up to her creed—by exposing parts of her body. "I was wearing a pink *chima-chogori* [a traditional Korean dress], which I had bought in North Korea. While singing karaoke in front to the guys, I flashed the part covering my chest, one side at a time. I wasn't wearing a bra. I had a lot of alcohol in me, so I did the same thing with the bottom part, and I wasn't wearing any panties."

Aoyama claims it was all part of an effort to thaw Japanese-North Korean relations. "We have a lot of issues, such as the abductions and nuclear weapons. However, if we just stop talking to each other, we'll never able to solve anything," she says. (GB)

DEATH IN SADDLE ONE OF MANY

Shukan Post (November 21, 2003)

Masahiko Ueno, a former director of the Medical Examiner's Office, has carried out autopsies on more than 20,000 bodies during a career spanning more than half a century. Of all those cases, one in particular stands out sharply in his mind. The incident occurred in a hotel room in the mid-1950s.

"A man and a woman had died just as they were having sex," Ueno recalls. "The woman was underneath, the man on top. In this case, they had both drunk cyanide right in the middle of their lovemaking.

"Normally when people commit suicide using cyanide, they never die in a perfect embrace like these two had," he tells *Shukan Post*. That was due to a series of odd coincidences at the site, he says. For one, the lovers had bound themselves together with cord, and also they had been pressed down under the weight of a particularly heavy futon. Consequently, the bodies had been prevented from contorting and managed to maintain the positions the couple had been in at their height of passion. It was a startling scene—they looked like lovers frozen in time.

The suicide was one of 176 cases that Ueno investigated involving people who died during the throes of passion. The doctor recalls them in his book, titled *The Sad Deaths of Men and Women*.

The reader learns that about half the deaths examined by Ueno involved married couples, and the vast majority of victims, about 85 percent of the total, were men. The overwhelming majority of the victims died from heart-related problems. Yet it was a different story for the women, who tended to die from brain hemorrhages.

But perhaps a more surprising set of statistics concerns the victims' ages. Many would assume that old men would be especially vulnerable to dying in such a state of bliss. In fact, the most common age bracket for both men and women was the 30s, followed by the 40s, 50s, 20s and then 60s.

"Lots of people in their 30s and 40s are busy doing things that tend to trigger stress," Ueno explains. "However these people still have their strength and vigor so they feel no need to adjust their lifestyles properly or take any preventative health measures. Before they know it, they're on their way to a heart attack or brain hemorrhage."

And not all were couples. Quite a few died alone. One perished while in the toilet cubicle of a strip club, evidently after being inspired by what he had just seen on stage. Another was a Peeping Tom who had climbed a telephone pole late one night for a glimpse through the bedroom window of an amorous young couple. As he attempted to transfer his grip from one pole to another, he plunged to his death.

"The things we learn from people who die can contribute greatly to the field of preventative medicine," Ueno says. "That's why I compiled and analyzed these statistics." (GB)

There's a famous fairy tale in which a handsome prince in search of a bride succeeds in differentiating a true princess from several pretenders by having each of them spend a night on a mattress under which he has placed a single pea. The impostors sleep through the night without discomfort; the real princess comes down the next morning red-eyed, complaining about how the lumpy mattress kept her awake all night.

Based on such criteria, it's clear that the 12 ladies who frequented a love hotel in Kyoto were definitely not of royal blood: They and their male partners, reports *Shukan Jitsuwa*, made love on a mattress unaware that the corpse of a dead woman had been placed underneath.

The existence of the body in a room at the hotel, in Kyoto's Higashiyama district, came to light on February 19. The body, which was completely nude except for pink rubber hairbands around the wrist, bore no signs of violence, and no other possessions, such as clothing or a handbag, were found. According to police, the cause of death from the results of a forensic autopsy was not clear, but she tested negative for drugs. The body was eventually identified as that of Yukari Inoue, a 28-year-old singer and karaoke instructor, and police are investigating the case as a murder.

"The mattress was one of those types that drop into the frame," a member of Kyoto Prefectural Police Headquarters tells the magazine. "Her corpse made some bumps in the mattress, but none of the couples who used the bed paid much attention. When the maid was changing the sheets, she finally noticed the mattress was bulging, which was caused by bloating of the corpse. She called the hotel manager and he found the body."

Inoue is believed to have been killed during the early morning hours of February 11. At least 12 couples had made use of the room, and presumably the bed, during the period between her death and the body's discovery. Lending, *Shukan Jitsuwa* suggests, tongue-in-cheek, a completely new meaning to such moans of ecstasy as, "Oh god, I'm coming!"

According to Inoue's father, they had been cut off in the midst of their last telephone conversation on February 7. Telephone records indicate no calls had been made or received from the night of February 10 onwards. A keen-eared neighbor in the same building reported hearing a woman enter Inoue's apartment in the very late hours on the night of February 17. The same person left 10 minutes later, apparently wearing a different pair of shoes.

After graduation from high school, Inoue worked for an electronics company in Maizuru city, but quit her job after about six weeks. She never remained long at her subsequent jobs. She had been living at her final address for the past four years. In the course of investigating her background, *Shukan Jitsuwa* also discovered that Inoue had been married—for only one day. For now, her life remains as much of a mystery as her death. (MS)

ACKNOWLEDGEMENTS

This book has been a team effort from start to finish, and its authors readily acknowledge the many individuals who made it possible.

First, to the management and staff of the *Japan Times*, with particular thanks to our friends and colleagues in the Arts & Entertainment Department, past and present, including Masaru Fujimoto, Tai Kawabata, Andrew Kershaw and Mark Thompson. And, of course, to the three editors of the Media Page where "Tokyo Confidential" has appeared since its inception in April 2001: Stephanie Coop, Rowan Hooper and Simon Bartz. To other *JT* editorial staff who lent their assistance and advice, including Victoria James, Payal Kapadia, Irma Nunez and Rob Hong. And to our always-supportive neighbor on the page, columnist Philip Brasor.

The authors also recognize their longstanding debt of gratitude to the Mainichi Shimbun-sha, parent company of the *Mainichi Daily News*, and the latter's past and present staff, particularly Hiroyuki Ono and Greg Mettam.

To Greg Starr and the staff of Kodansha International: Thank you for believing in us and working so hard to make this book happen.

And last, but certainly not least, we extend our deepest bows of respect to the hardworking writers and editors of the Japanese vernacular magazines that have served as the sources of our columns these many years. *"Taihen otsukaresama deshita."*

ABOUT THE AUTHORS

GEOFF BOTTING is a Canadian who has lived in Japan since graduating from the University of Victoria in 1986. He has worked as a journalist for *the Mainichi Daily News*, The *Japan Times,* NHK, the national broadcaster, and the Kyodo News Agency. He lives in Tokyo.

Australian RYANN CONNELL works for the Mainichi newspaper, specializing in stories about unseen Japan. A resident of Tokyo for almost 20 years, he idolizes his daughters, Misha and Natasha, fertility festivals and raw horse flesh-flavored ice cream.

MICHAEL HOFFMAN, originally from Montreal, Canada, is a freelance writer and translator living in Otaru, Hokkaido. He is the author of three books of fiction, the latest being *The Coat that Covers Him and Other Stories* (Authorhouse 2004).

A newspaper and magazine columnist, translator and author, MARK SCHREIBER has lived in Asia since 1965 and currently makes his home in Tokyo. He is author of *The Dark Side: Infamous Japanese Crimes and Criminals* (Kodansha International, 2001).

（英文版）タブロイド・トーキョー
Tabloid Tokyo

2005 年 6 月27日　第 1 刷発行

著　者　　マーク・シュライバー、ジェフ・ボテイング、
　　　　　ライアン・コネル、マイケル・ホフマン
発行者　　畑野文夫
発行所　　講談社インターナショナル株式会社
　　　　　〒112-8652
　　　　　東京都文京区音羽 1-17-14
　　　　　電話 03-3944-6493（編集部）
　　　　　　　　03-3944-6492（営業部・業務部）
　　　　　ホームページ　www.kodansha-intl.com

印刷・製本所　大日本印刷株式会社